Permission to Believe

Permission to Believe

Finding Faith in Troubled Times

SAMUEL E. KARFF

ABINGDON PRESS / Nashville

PERMISSION TO BELIEVE
FINDING FAITH IN TROUBLED TIMES

Copyright © 2005 by Samuel Egal Karff

This book is printed on acid-free paper.

Library of Congress Cataloging-in-Publication Data

Karff, Samuel E.
    Permission to believe : finding faith in troubled times / Samuel E. Karff.
        p. cm.
    Includes bibliographical references.
    ISBN 0-687-32539-0 (binding: pbk.: alk. paper)
    1. Faith. 2. Belief and doubt. I. Title.

BV4637.K37 2005
296.7—dc22

                                                                    2004026326

All Scripture is from *The TANAKH: The New JPS Translation According to the Traditional Hebrew Text.* Copyright © 1985 by the Jewish Publication Society. Used by permission.

Quotations on pages 9, 28, and 193 from David Polish, ed., *Rabbi's Manual* (New York: Central Conference of American Rabbis, 1988) are used by permission.

05 06 07 08 09 10 11 12 13 14—10 9 8 7 6 5 4 3 2 1

MANUFACTURED IN THE UNITED STATES OF AMERICA

Contents

Preface / vii

Acknowledgments / xi

Introduction / 1

1. What Is Faith? / 9

2. What Kind of Life Is This Anyway? / 23

3. Confronting the Obstacles to Faith / 35

4. Recovering Faith—
A Guide to a Deeper Spirituality / 49

5. Prayer—The Vital Connection / 71

6. Overcoming a Crisis of Faith / 93

7. When Prayer Is Not Enough / 109

8. The Power of Love / 127

9. Living in a Broken World / 143

10. Sustaining Faith in Our Later Years / 161

11. Dance, Laughter, and Hope / 177

Notes / 201

Preface

IN MY FORTY YEARS as a congregational rabbi, I have had many encounters with people who would cast me as a "defender of the faith." Often such discussions became intense, at times even confrontational. Sometimes people would explain to me that they are atheists or at best agnostics because no one can "prove" that there is a God. Some would confess that they were once fervent believers until a devastating personal trauma convinced them of the randomness and inherent meaninglessness of life. Others felt that discarding the consolations of religion and other security blankets of childhood marked the dawn of their maturity.

In virtually all such discussions, however, I discovered that on some level my challengers wanted me to win the argument. Even if they didn't feel they could embrace the religious view of life, many wished they could. They pressed their nonbelief against my faith with an intensity that betrayed a deep longing for permission to believe.

We seek such permission because, periodically, our human experience cries out for a spiritual interpretation. Those moments when we feel graced by unearned gifts call forth the irrepressible prayer—"Thank God" or "Thank goodness." At difficult times in life, even avowed atheists and agnostics have been known to pray to a God they do not formally acknowledge. When life circumstances seem desperate, with no sign of deliverance, and something happens or someone appears just in time to reopen the window of hope, the word "coincidence" seems inadequate. When we have to face the death of a loved one, we ask, "Is this all there is?" and something within us may insist that we are more than a whisper of dust.

Granting ourselves permission to believe does not require that we turn away from the "ordinary world" but that we heed these deep intuitions of our heart. To do so requires no surrender of our respect for science or our sophistication. It requires only an understanding that much of our most significant human experiences cannot be described or explained through the language of science. Life is not only a puzzle to solve, but also a mystery to embrace.

Granting ourselves permission to believe does not mean that we need to repress our moments of honest doubt. Many of the great religious spirits of all ages have acknowledged that there is a believer and an unbeliever in each of us. But as we shall see, there is a world of difference between accommodating doubt within a life of faith and making doubt or disbelief the dominant mode of one's life.

For yet another reason denial of belief is an uncomfortable resting place. Martin Buber, the great twentieth-century religious thinker, tells the story of Rabbi Levi of Berditchev. One day a man who was both intellectually astute and a confirmed atheist traveled to Berditchev to confront the rabbi. He hoped to undermine the rabbi's ground for belief. When the atheist appeared at the rabbi's home he found Rabbi Levi pacing back and forth, completely absorbed in thought. He paid no attention to his guest for what seemed like an eternity. Finally, Rabbi Levi stopped, paused, and then addressed his guest, "My son, the great Torah scholars with whom you debated, wasted their words on you. When you left them you only laughed at what they had said. They could not set God and his kingdom on the table before you, and I cannot do this either. But, my son, only think! Perhaps it is true." The impassioned nonbeliever was shaken and disarmed by those words.[1]

Our yearning to believe is fed by the possibility that the claims of religious faith are true after all, and by the sense that those who live with a religious support system are better able to embrace life in its totality without cynicism or despair.

I am writing this book for people who want to deepen the role of faith in their lives. My intent is not to write a brief for any one religion, but to contend that religious faith is the most profound response to the wonders and trauma of life. When I speak of religion I am talking about a liberal faith that charts a course between fundamentalism on the right and an amorphous spirituality on the left. Such faith values tradition for its multiple, sometimes conflicting answers to life's deepest questions. It is strong enough to shape the way we live, yet humble enough to respect the religious quest of others.

This book is meant to be a source of encouragement to those who recoil from religious extremism and the havoc it creates in the world but who still long for permission to believe in a personal God because of a deep need for transcendent meaning in their lives. At its best, that is what religion is all about.

I bring to these pages my own faith struggle, the experience of people I have known, and the stories of my tradition. As a student and teacher of sacred texts, I have found that many of these biblical, talmudic, and Hasidic stories speak to me and others I have counseled with a powerful resonance. These are, after all, stories of human beings grappling with the enigmas of life, the tragedies of their own times, their personal, spiritual, and family crises, and their human quest for meaning. These texts of faith reflect thousands of years of human spiritual yearnings.

Although I draw largely from my own tradition, the basic issues of belief and faith transcend any particular heritage. Faith is always personal—a personal opening up to whatever affirms the ultimate value of our lives. My goal is to bring these insights from the Jewish tradition into the general discussion of reconnecting to faith in our times. I write with the hope that this book will be useful to anyone who seeks to discover or recover faith in a world that is broken.

Acknowledgments

THIS BOOK HAS ENGAGED my mind and soul many summer mornings at our little cottage by the lake. At the end of each summer I put the manuscript aside until our return to Charlevoix. Meeting my preaching, teaching, and pastoral responsibilities did not leave time or energy to spend on the book during the intervening months. Therefore, my writing and revisions extended over more years than I care to count.

During this time, I received much assistance, counsel, and support. A generous grant from the David and Mary Wolff Foundation covered my expenses during the book's preparation for publication.

Joan Mag Karff, my life partner and dearest friend, read the various drafts with a critical eye and steadfast encouragement. Rachel Karff Weissenstein, my daughter the English teacher, read a number of chapters and gave me her insightful response. She and her sisters, Amy Karff Halevy and Elizabeth Karff Kampf, have been an inspiration for much of my work.

Bonny Fetterman, a gifted editor who became a cherished friend, provided invaluable assistance. Bonny believed in the book even when she unsparingly critiqued it.

Tom Cole, distinguished teacher of medical humanities, fine writer, and friend read an earlier draft and made helpful suggestions.

Vickie Burnett has been by my side during much of this project as secretary, administrative assistant, and amazing retriever of sources. She lovingly typed various revisions of the manuscript and reassured me that it also speaks to her, a believing Christian.

Catherine Beer, my devoted secretary for many years, typed the early drafts and was among the project's earliest supporters.

Rabbi Elaine Glickman identified and checked many of the rabbinic references.

All the above have made this a better book. I alone am responsible for its shortcomings.

Introduction

DURING MY SECOND YEAR at Harvard, I realized that I no longer wanted to be a lawyer. I had decided upon graduation to enter seminary and become a rabbi. When my mother heard the news, she informed me that we were descendants of Rabbi Pinhas Shapiro of Koretz. Neither she nor I knew much about our eighteenth-century ancestor. At the time I did not venture to discover the man behind the name.

Years later while a student at Hebrew Union College, I visited Israel as an adult for the first time. My grandmother, Manya, who lived in Jerusalem, had last seen me when I was a three-year-old. Now I was twenty-three and she was in her late seventies, a petite, frail, pretty woman with a moon-shaped face, smooth skin, and a radiant smile. I remember her embrace and her tears. I also remember her unmistakable perplexity when I told her I was studying to be a rabbi. In my khaki pants and T-shirt, I surely did not match the profile of rabbis she knew in Jerusalem or her image of Rabbi Pinhas, our famous ancestor.

Grandmother Manya was herself several generations removed from Pinhas but her Orthodox piety linked her more directly to his world than mine. Hearing my vocational plans, Manya did not express bewilderment or disapproval. She simply smiled in acknowledgment of another dimension of modern life that eluded her understanding. How incomprehensible it must have seemed to her that her grandchild, the rabbinic student, a descendant of Pinhas of Koretz, was so unrabbinic in appearance and observance.

I visited Israel again after I was ordained. By then, Grandmother Manya had managed to integrate my dual identity as grandson and rabbi. On this, our last encounter before her death, Manya gave me a Bible with this Hebrew inscription: "To my grandson, *Rabbi* Samuel Karff." That Bible with the inscription acknowledging my rabbinic status was precious validation—the equivalent of giving me her blessing.

Eventually, my vague curiosity about Rabbi Pinhas ripened into a quest for more knowledge. I read Martin Buber's *Tales of the Hasidim: The Early Masters* and found an entire chapter devoted to my ancestor. Pinhas was born in 1728 in the Polish village of Shklov but was generally linked to the town of Koretz ("Korzec" in Polish). Pinhas was a young contemporary of Rabbi Israel, known as the Baal Shem Tov ("Master of the Good Name"), the charismatic founder of the Hasidism. He might well have been Rabbi Israel's successor but he evidently shunned the mantle of leadership and turned instead to a life of study and meditation.

My world—which already differs so from the world of my grandmother Manya—seems light years away from the world of our eighteenth-century ancestor Pinhas of Koretz. Surely my liberal Judaism distances me from his scrupulous observance of traditional Jewish law. Even greater are the cultural differences between living in eighteenth-century Poland and twenty-first-century America. When Pinhas admonished his disciples not to seek medical therapy from Gentiles or women, he was reflecting the cultural chasm between us. Pinhas knew nothing of the separation of church and state, or political democracy and pluralism, or the kind of relationships I enjoy with Christians. He, of course, also knew nothing of modern high-tech medicine or the Internet.

Still, I share his need to make sense of a world of incredible beauty and so much pain, his need to come to terms with the grandeur and pathos of human life, and most of all, his quest for meaning through faith in a God who is the Source of our being, a guiding, healing presence in our lives—and yet at times so hidden.

In spite of his shyness and humility, the respect and admiration Pinhas inspired drew people to him for comfort and counsel. In his book *Somewhere a Master,* Elie Wiesel tells the story of a troubled man who came to Rabbi Pinhas to confide his distress and despair. Disappointed by the false words and deeds of those around him, this young man was also overwhelmed by the sadness in his own life and the lives of people he knew. His faith in a just and merciful God who is creator and sovereign of the world was crumbling. Nothing seemed to make sense.

When Rabbi Pinhas suggested that the young man study Torah and Talmud, he replied that his deep anguish and uncertainty made him unable to study. At that point Pinhas drew closer to the young man and said:

You must know, my friend, that what is happening to you also happened to me. . . . I, too, was filled with questions and doubts. About man and his fate, creation and its meaning. . . . I was wallowing in doubt, locked in despair. I tried study, prayer, meditation, . . . penitence, silence, solitude. My doubts remained doubts. Worse: they became threats. Impossible to proceed. . . . I simply could not go on. Then one day I learned that [Rabbi] Israel Baal Shem Tov would be coming to our town. Curiosity led me to the [synagogue], where he was receiving his followers. I entered just as he was finishing the *Amida* prayer. He turned around and saw me, and I was convinced that he was seeing me, me and no one else. The intensity of his gaze overwhelmed me, and I felt less alone. And strangely, I was able to go home, open the Talmud, and plunge into my studies once more. You see, . . . the questions remained questions. But I was able to go on.[1]

This story resonates within me, for I too live with unresolved questions. I was relieved to discover that a great, pious rabbinic ancestor also had his questions and doubts. And, like Pinhas, I was able to carry on and move beyond these periods, not because of compelling arguments that neatly dissolved all my perplexity, but because of people who entered my life in time of need, and whose love and genuine concern became for me intimations of God's love and concern. I left their presence able to reaffirm my faith that beyond the mystery there is meaning.

What is more, I have been privileged at times to give the same gift to a troubled congregant that Pinhas gave the young man who came to him, and which he himself had received from Rabbi Israel the Baal Shem Tov. With all that radically separates me from my ancestor, each of us found his sacred vocation in being a rabbi. And for me, as for him, the meaning found in a religious view of life remains the only adequate response to the human condition.

André Malraux was France's Minister in Charge of Cultural Affairs. His friend had spent fifteen years as a parish priest. The two men spoke late into the night. Malraux asked the priest what he had learned from hearing all those confessions. The priest replied, "First of all, people are much more unhappy than one thinks . . . and then . . . the fundamental fact is that *there is no such thing as a grown-up person.*"[2]

The first proposition hardly needs elaboration. Whatever our century, in this world none of us will be spared life's tragic dimension. But what of the second proposition—that there is no such thing as a grown-up? We associate growing up with shedding childish dependence on parents or guardians, a readiness to face the world alone, if necessary, and be self-reliant. When we grow up we are expected to abandon childish notions and replace fantasy with reason. And in the modern world, many equate maturity with the need to discard belief in a God who cannot be proved by the standards of reason and science.

For Sigmund Freud, growing up meant to discard the illusion that life has some transcendent meaning. Freud contended that religious believers, neither strong nor mature enough to shed such childish illusions, fantasize a world responsive to their deepest wishes. They need a meaningful world and so they imagine or conjure such a world into existence.

Such psychologizing by Freud or others does not, however, settle the basic issue: Is the age-old fascination with a power and presence within and beyond the surface of life simply a defensive reaction to our own fear and powerlessness, or is it a response to a genuine reality? Do we seek God only because we are weak, or because God is seeking us? That we need God is not grounds to conclude that God is unreal. That need tells us nothing about whether God exists. Attempts to resolve the issue of God's existence by appealing to psychological arguments ultimately take us nowhere.

So, what does André Malraux's priest friend mean when he says, "There is no such thing as a grown-up person"? I think he means that the profoundest sign of maturity is to realize that in some inescapable way we are all as vulnerable as children. It has been said that the difference between children and adults is the expense of their toys. I would add—and the nature of their security blankets. As adults, our toys may include the automobile in the garage or our wardrobe or our sophisticated computer software. Our security blankets may include the titles we place after our name, the degrees we have earned, the mastery of a technical language in our profession that sets us apart and makes us feel superior to the uninitiated. Our security blankets may be the wealth and power we wield over others.

I take the priest's assertion not as an indictment of our failure to leave childhood behind, but as an assertion of our essential humanity. We must all die and bad things often happen to good people and each life inevitably has its share of defeats and disappointments. Yet we seek the meaning of our brief journey in this world and we ask, what can we rely on in the face of life's encompassing mystery? What is the foundation of our conviction that life is worthwhile? We are children because we never lose the sense that we are limited and finite beings. At some point, we must confront the inadequacy of all our toys and security blankets. We each must acknowledge that our mortality is not a problem to be solved but a reality to accept.

I know a very competent and successful attorney who is scrupulously analytical and rational in his approach to life. Recently, he was confronted with a life-threatening illness. My friend confided to me with some astonishment that in his anxiety he conjured the image of his deceased parents. When he asked them for support, he actually felt their presence. After my friend relayed this strange experience, I suggested that despite all our pretensions or aspirations to the contrary, in some existential sense we all remain children. Invoking his deceased parents was but a short step away from praying. The natural human response to the fearful and awesome awareness of our essential vulnerability is prayer—to reach out to a divine parent.

In different but similar ways, Malraux's priest friend and Rabbi Pinhas staked their lives on the affirmation that, despite its darker side, life is a precious gift imbued with meaning—and we are not alone. Despite moments of doubt and anguish, they found a way to internalize a life-affirming option called faith.

After Pinhas's first encounter with Rabbi Israel the Baal Shem Tov, he met with him privately and the master told him, "Man is not alone." Undoubtedly those words helped Pinhas carry on despite the unresolved questions and the lingering doubts. The resonance of those words has sustained me as well. These four words point to a Presence who gives us life, who cares how we live it, and who is the foundation of our deepest hopes.

Do we believe we are not alone only because we remain children who need to believe? Are we nurturing what Freud would have called a wish-fulfilling fantasy? My faith is nourished not only by my need but also by intimations of God's presence in my personal life. Those intimations come from spirit-filled persons who have touched my life, from opening myself to the awesome wonders of this world, from the sacred stories of my heritage, and from moments of meditation and prayer.

To acknowledge our needfulness does not make us children. As adults, we want to learn and grow in wisdom. As the psalmist prays, "Teach us to count our days rightly, / that we may obtain a wise heart" (Psalm 90:12). But part of maturity may be in recognizing that we are not self-sufficient. The needs of the heart are wired into us as firmly as our intellectual aspirations. Our adult defenses and pretensions do not serve us well when they block our instinctive need to connect. Here is when faith can help us, by showing us how to recover that ability we had as children—to reach for and respond to love.

Chapter 1

What Is Faith?

"We praise you, O God, Judge of truth."
—Rabbi's Manual

A RABBI'S GREATEST PRIVILEGE is to enter people's lives at moments of peak joy and deep sorrow. Through the years I have led celebrants in the traditional prayers of gratitude for a child's birth or coming of age or a couple's marriage. At such moments I have helped them experience the God who is the giver of precious gifts. But I have felt most needed when good people have experienced life's darker side. Once their world of order and meaning has been shaken, conflicting sentiments overwhelm them. They need to express their quarrel with life and with God but they also want to recover their love of life and to draw comfort and hope from life's ultimate Source.

Such encounters foster the deepest bonds between the rabbi and the family. The traumatic events that have befallen the family make my own faith a struggle rather than an easy possession. And yet I emerge from such pastoral moments more certain than ever that a religious perspective is the most compelling response to the highs and lows of the human condition.

To be sure, God does not always make it easy to believe. The Jewish mystics compare God to the rays of the sun

9

reflected on the water's surface: radiant but not graspable, elusive, darting in and out of consciousness. There are times that sorely strain our power to believe because there is so much suffering we don't deserve. And some of the nicest people can be assaulted by life's toughest scenarios. At times, faith challenges us to believe in spite of what has happened to us or those we love.

My Hasidic ancestor, Rabbi Pinhas, alluded to such faith. Once his favorite disciple, Rabbi Raphael, complained to Pinhas that in adversity it is so difficult to feel or believe in God's loving presence. At such times it seems that God's face is hidden. "What shall one do to strengthen faith?" he asked. Pinhas replied, "It ceases to be a hiding if you know it is a hiding."[1] It ceases to be a hiding if on some level we believe God is real, that God cares for us, and that there is some meaning in the mystery of life.

Times of crisis, I have often found, contain within them the seeds of renewed faith. In those difficult moments I question but cling to my faith because, while it is not always easy to live with God, I have not found it possible to live without God.

It has been three years since Jack and Linda's son died. He was seven and a half years old; a brawny, handsome, bright, impish, and loving child who was last seen vibrantly alive when his father asked him to retrieve a tool from the family camper parked in the driveway. Minutes later Nicholas lay unconscious under a heavy board that had fallen and crushed him. He did not regain consciousness.

I visited with Jack and Linda in the ICU that afternoon. We cried and prayed together next to Nicholas's hospital bed. A day later I was summoned in the middle of the night. The doctors had removed the respirator and Jack and Linda needed to say good-bye to their son. Then in her eighth month of pregnancy, Linda was struggling between her deepest grief over Nicholas and the need to care for herself and protect the life she was carrying. The image of Jack holding his son in his arms, trying to speak as he audibly thanked Nicholas for all he had given them, will remain etched in my memory as long as I live.

In the days that followed, my rabbinic colleagues and I spent many hours with the family. Numbing shock gave way to an acute awareness of their unfathomable loss. I encouraged their parents and grandparents, aunts and uncles and friends to share their stories about Nicholas. We cried and we laughed through our tears as we spoke of this remarkable child's impact on his family and peers in such a short life. At the graveside service I spoke about their memories of Nicholas:

> Nicholas had heroes who did not fail him. At Hero Day at school, when Nicholas said his hero was his dad, he described a dad who taught him to be kind and to care and who took him fishing and hunting. . . . He did lots of chores to help pay for his karate lessons and other stuff. At an early age he had the satisfaction of earning some of life's treats. So many of us do not receive that satisfaction until we are much older. Nicholas not only enjoyed an ideal childhood; he bestowed precious gifts on many persons of all ages. He was a great mentor to his younger brother Daniel. He mentored his own parents by expecting them to practice the standards they taught him. He was full of fun and a practical joker. . . . Nicholas was strong, sweet, and incredibly sensitive—a gift from his mother. When his maternal grandfather had died and his mother took him to school, each day she broke into tears along the way. Nicholas asked, "Why are you crying?" Linda explained she was weeping because his grandfather had died. "Can you understand?" Nicholas replied feelingly, "Sure, Mom, he was your dad, he was your father." Would anyone who knew Nicholas doubt he is among those our sages speak of as acquiring a claim to eternal life in a single moment?

More than a hundred people huddled around the grave as psalms were chanted and the cantor sang the *El Maley Rachamim*, a prayer entrusting Nicholas's soul to God. His parents recited the Kaddish, the mourner's prayer that proclaims trust in God even in the midst of grievous loss.

In the months ahead, numbness and bitter grieving would slowly give way to some healing. The need to help surviving son Daniel cope with the new reality and the demands of the newborn Michael helped distract and soothe Linda and Jack's aching hearts. But Nicholas's absence left a gaping hole.

No doubt the loving embrace of our religious community and Nicholas's teachers at our day school and the caring attention of family and friends eased the suffering. Whether Nicholas's death was a random event in God's world or part of a plan beyond our understanding, Linda and Jack would never know. But they needed to believe that Nicholas was in a safe place with God, the God whose embracing love Linda and Jack desperately needed for themselves to carry on with their lives.

The recovery of faith was a struggle over time. In the days following the funeral Jack and Linda recited the mourner's prayer but, as Jack told me, it was an empty exercise and the worship services he dutifully attended "were gray and meaningless."

Although the death of Nicholas sorely challenged my own faith, I stood at the grave in the presence of family and friends and recited the appropriate prayers, but my heart was not fully in it. I could barely suppress the silent cry, "Why, God, is life so unfair?"—yet I proceeded to utter the prescribed words, "Praised be Thou, O God whose judgments are true."

Does embracing these opposites of doubt and faith make me a hypocrite? What would my rabbinic ancestors say, including Rabbi Pinhas? For him, too, spiritual struggle was the price of living with a God who is both hidden and revealed. Fortunately, like Pinhas, I have experienced many times the stunning beauty of God's gifts and the bracing nearness of God's healing presence. I sense that presence at times as I stand in front of our summer cottage and watch the morning sunrise over the lake or when, on a clear night, I peer at the stars. Or while I sit at my desk to write an essay, and the words that had eluded my blank mind suddenly gush forth out of the void. Then I newly appreciate the words of gratitude in the traditional prayer, "Praised are You, O God, . . . giver of knowledge."

In times of illness I have prayed for and I have often experienced healing of body or spirit or both. In times of trouble I have often felt I was not alone. When I felt trapped by circumstances or conditions beyond my control, I have at times been surprised by new possibilities; and in the midst of losses that were irreversible, I was given the power to get up the next morning and face a new day with courage and hope. As a rabbi I have taught the wisdom of a tradition that does not blink at the stark realities of this world and yet continually reaffirms the preciousness of this life.

Since I use the words "meaning" and "healing" almost interchangeably, let me define them and suggest their relationship to each other. Many years ago psychiatrist Viktor Frankl concluded that the human will to live is not instinctive; it can be lost. Witness the phenomenon of suicide. But this will to live can be sustained even under the most terrible circumstances if something within the mind and soul endows life—then and there—with meaning. In the simplest terms, "meaning" is the assurance that, even when we are confronted by its darker side, life is worth living; it is the sense that our life has a purpose beyond the satisfaction of those needs we share with the animal kingdom. Meaning is what enables us to endure and transcend even the painful physical or social conditions of our present existence.

Frankl himself was a survivor of Auschwitz. In his book *Man's Search for Meaning,* he describes one of a series of torturous marches under frigid conditions when death seemed more inviting to him than life. What enabled Frankl to cling to life? He was sustained by the mental image of his beloved wife, a prisoner in another camp, by his hope that she was still alive and that they would be reunited. "My mind clung to my wife's image, imagining it with an uncanny acuteness. I heard her answering me, saw her smile, her frank and encouraging look. Real or not, her look was then more luminous than the sun which was beginning to rise."[2]

Although most of us have been spared such extreme circumstances, all of us have known periods of physical or emotional suffering. For us, too, recovering the will to live requires some purpose or set of goals that can fully absorb our minds and mobilize our energy.

In the absence of serious illness or terrible loss or crises of confidence most of us don't routinely ask the "big question." But when the order in our world unravels—the question always intrudes. We need desperately to move beyond the chaos of the moment and reaffirm our belief in the goodness of life. Those who have gone to the doctor and heard the words "you have cancer" know that challenge. So does the spouse whose mate suddenly decides to leave the marriage. At such times we need somehow to hold on to a sense of meaning in our lives. To do so is ultimately an act of faith.

When we think of healing we conjure the image of medical specialists or psychotherapists who will cure us of our illness or at least alleviate the physical and emotional pain. At their best, such clinicians are indeed healers and we should be exceedingly grateful for the advances in the battle against diseases that afflict body and mind and for those with the skill and knowledge to cure us. But to be healed is more encompassing than to be *cured.*

Healing has a spiritual dimension. My friend Ronny spent the last eighteen months of his life with ALS, the progressively debilitating and incurable neurological disorder also known as Lou Gehrig's disease. When Ronny was already confined to a wheelchair and in need of being bathed, dressed, and fed by others, he surprised me by remarking, "I am the same person in a different body." I think we all knew that, but his comment revealed that Ronny remained conscious of a core self—his personhood—that included but transcended his body. Broken in body, he remained amazingly well in spirit. Ronny continued to appear at public events and sustained his interest in family and friends. When he could hardly speak he whispered, "I am not ready to give up." He still cherished life and was sustained by the hope that the One who brought him into this world would be with him through his difficult journey, and in the world beyond.

To be healed in spirit is to retain or recover an inner well-being in the midst of physical disability or illness or in the aftermath of a tragedy. It is to feel that the present circumstances, however difficult and challenging, cannot divest life of goodness or meaning. Meaning and healing are inextricably bound together. We can experience healing without being cured of our disease but we cannot be fully healed without having recovered a sense of life's meaning. Conversely, some persons who are free of disease or illness in the narrower sense are still not well. They are cured without being healed. Both meaning and healing require a compelling vision of wholeness and well-being in the midst of life's brokenness.

In recent years physicians and psychotherapists have rediscovered the interdependence of mind, body, and spirit.

Moreover, clinical research documents that those who manage to sustain a sense of life's goodness suffer less from their pain and are more likely to contribute to their own recovery. We are also rediscovering that a physician who offers not only medical knowledge but also a caring sensitivity and a respect for the patient's dignity is likely to be a more effective healer of the body.

As a congregational rabbi I have seen the contribution of religious faith, prayer, ritual, and sacred story to a healing of the body. Not all sickness can be cured; not all that is broken in life can be fixed. The body may be racked with incurable disease or assaulted by the losses of aging. But many who have been wounded by life have found ways to live with love, joy, and hope.

Some of what I share in this book are the sources of my own faith, culled from the stories in the Jewish Wisdom literature; much has been tested in the crucible of my own encounter with life's trials. While I consider myself incredibly blessed, in these pages I write of my struggle to overcome depression, of a devastating fire that completely destroyed our family home of twenty years, of my battle with prostate cancer, and of other health crises that needed to be overcome in the life of my family. I write not only as an empathetic observer of another's pain. I know firsthand that to live is to suffer, to be wounded and to need healing. Most of the inspiration for this book, however, comes from my encounter with persons like Ronny, Jack, and Linda, whose courage and dignity under severe trial have deeply moved me and strengthened my own belief in the healing power of faith.

What is faith? When I counsel people trying to recover from the traumas of life, I find myself teaching through stories. Most people are moved more by story than by formal theology. In my years of weekly sermons, the congregation's attention was far more engaged when I told stories than when I tried to expound abstract theology. In the Jewish tradition such stories are called *Aggadah*. In this book I use the term to embrace both the narratives of the Bible and the stories that emerge from the religious imagination and experience of the ancient rabbis recorded in the Talmud and Midrash. These stories often address the deepest questions of life. Their beauty lies in the fact that they are open-ended and speak to us on a variety of levels. They give us new paradigms for thinking about our place in the world. These stories both respect the ultimate mystery of our existence and illuminate it.

Spiritual truth is best approached through story and metaphor. That is why *Aggadah* is anthropomorphic. In moments when God has been most real to me I have felt addressed and obligated, accountable and judged. I have also felt loved, forgiven, blessed. That which can exercise such a claim or evoke my faithful response is best imagined as a person. We use story and metaphor even as we know that God is beyond all our stories. These narratives are the least inadequate way for us humans to describe our faith.

Great religious stories are preserved in sacred texts and passed on from generation to generation. These narratives become the lens of faith through which we perceive our world.

In my effort to comfort Jack and Linda I would in time share with them some of our tradition's stories. The time for such sharing would only come months after Nicholas's death. In the freshness of loss they needed unconditional love, not theology or even the stories that embody our faith. At first Jack and Linda's need to grieve was all-consuming. In time they were ready to sort out the broken pieces of life's puzzle and search for sources of strength. When they asked me, "Rabbi, how could God let this happen?" I turned with them to the stories from our tradition that deal precisely with this issue.

Where is God when terrible things happen? One cluster of stories drawn from biblical and rabbinic texts proclaims a self-limiting God—a God who created human beings with free will and a natural world that is governed by dependable laws. The Cain and Abel story deals with free will. God warns Cain that while his grievances may trigger an urge to violence, "You may rule over it." The rest is up to Cain. Cain did not "rule over it," we read in Genesis; he murdered his brother.

In the Talmud, Rabbi Simeon ben Yochai re-imagines the encounter of Cain with God. When God asked Cain, "Where is your brother?" Cain replied, "Am I my brother's keeper?" Rabbi Simeon adds to Cain's reply, "You are God, you have created man, it is your task to watch him, not mine. If I ought not to have done what I did, you could have prevented me from doing it."³ God does not answer. The price of human freedom is a degree of divine restraint even in situations where human beings abuse their power and freedom. To be truly free we must have the capacity even to defy God.

God is also self-limited by having created a world governed by natural laws. The Talmud relates the story of a man who stole a measure of wheat and sowed it in the ground. Those stolen seeds grew just as well as the wheat planted by the honest farmer across the road. The text tells us, "It is right that it should not grow, but the world pursues its natural course and as for the fools who act wrongly, they will have to render account [in the World-to-Come]."⁴ Not all that happens in God's world is in accordance with God's will. Similarly, a deadly virus can afflict saint and sinner alike and lightning does not spare the innocent. The world created by God, "follows its natural course" without regard to justice or fairness.

In his book *Guide for the Perplexed,* the great medieval rabbi and philosopher Moses Maimonides teaches that disease and decay of the body are not necessarily punishment for sin but may simply be the price we pay for being flesh and blood human beings who live in a natural world.[5] As embodied persons of flesh and blood we can feel enormous pleasure and intense pain. Such suffering is the price we pay for the blessings of creation.

The Talmud teaches that Rabbi Elisha ben Abuya actually lost his faith and abandoned Judaism because he was so troubled by God's seeming failure to dependably reward the just and punish the transgressors of God's laws. Once Rabbi Elisha saw a man climb a ladder to retrieve young birds from the nest. He did so only after shooing away the mother bird so she would be spared seeing the fate of her offspring. The man in the story was actually following the commandment prescribed in Deuteronomy 22:6-7, "If, along the road, you chance upon a bird's nest, in any tree or on the ground, with fledglings or eggs and the mother sitting over the fledglings or on the eggs, do not take the mother together with her young. Let the mother go, and take only the young in order that you may fare well and have a long life."

How was the pious man in this story rewarded for fulfilling God's commandment? The ladder he used to climb the tree collapsed and the man was killed. Upon witnessing this, Rabbi Elisha concluded, "There is no justice and no judge."[6] From that point on, Elisha could no longer function as a teacher of the faith and became a heretic.

Other sages tried to explain the incident. One concluded that the pious man will be rewarded but his reward is merely being deferred to another life—the World-to-Come. Rabbi Eliezer disagreed. He concluded that God did not directly cause the man's death. The ladder he chose to climb was just too rickety to support him.

This cluster of stories points to a God who is not directly responsible for all the evils in the world, a God who is self-limited for divine purposes. But, where is God in our hour of travail? According to this view, God shares our pain. God weeps with the grieving families when such ladders collapse or when a seven-year-old is killed in a "freak accident." God is the source of courage and strength to cope with the tragic dimension of life. God also appears through those human messengers who shower us with love and helpful deeds in our time of despair. God has given us minds to discover the laws of nature so we can find cures for disease and lessen the harm of natural disasters. God inspires and impels us to be partners in bringing justice to the oppressed of this world. God is also the source of hope that good will ultimately prevail over evil because the infinite God works through us and beyond us to fulfill God's dream for creation.

A second perspective on undeserved suffering is also found in biblical and talmudic stories. Such stories assume that the infinite God is the controlling power in nature and history. In this view, God's will is manifest and God's purposes are somehow being fulfilled even in those darker events that befall us. Though we cannot fully comprehend God's ways, we must trust that the One who is responsible for our joys and also our sorrows loves us and desires the good for us.

The classic biblical example of this perspective is the story of Job. Job is a righteous man who is afflicted by a series of devastating misfortunes. His friends, the "false comforters," suggest that Job may have deserved all that has come upon him, but Job knows he is innocent. He demands to confront his Creator directly and argue his case before God. God answers Job "from out of the whirlwind," but God's answer is a surprising rebuke that has nothing to do with Job's innocence or guilt, "Who is this who darkens counsel, / Speaking without knowledge? / Gird your loins like a man; / I will ask and you will inform Me. / Where were you when I laid the earth's foundations? / Speak if you have understanding" (Job 38:2-4). God reminds him of the vastness and grandeur of the universe God created. God's answer to the question "Why?" is that we humans pose questions beyond our power to know and understand. Job is granted his integrity. He did not suffer because he deserved to suffer, as his supposed friends were ready to conclude. But the mystery of God's ways remains beyond his human power to comprehend. He must trust that beyond the mystery there is meaning.

These stories of a God who is in control of the universe and whose ways must be trusted is also found in the talmudic *Aggadah* about Rabbi Meir and his wife Beruriah. While Rabbi Meir was teaching in the house of study on a Sabbath afternoon his two young sons died (we might call it crib death). What did their mother do? She put them both on a couch and spread a sheet over them. At the end of the Sabbath, Rabbi Meir returned home from the house of study and asked, "Where are my two sons?" Beruriah replied, "A while ago a man came and deposited something in my keeping. Now he has come back to claim what he left. Shall I return it to him or not?" Rabbi Meir said to his wife, "Is not one who holds a deposit required to return it to its owner?" She took Rabbi Meir by his hand, led him up to the chamber, and brought him near the couch. Then she pulled off the sheet that covered them, and he saw that both children lying on the couch were dead. He began to weep. Then Beruriah asked, "Did you not say to me that we are required to restore to the owner what is left with us in trust? 'The Lord gave, the Lord took. May the name of the Lord be blessed.' "[7]

When Jack and Linda felt ready to ask how Judaism could help them come to terms with Nicholas's tragic death I shared both perspectives drawn from *Aggadah*. A year after Nicholas's death I invited Jack to participate in the Yom

Kippur symposium. Speakers are asked to do some deep reflecting on their life experience. Jack described Nicholas's death and his long journey toward healing. He told the congregation of the struggle to rebuild his faith. He spoke of the rawness of grief and confessed that the Mourner's Prayer, by which we proclaim trust in God in the face of tragic loss, was in the beginning an empty exercise. As time passed however he began to find comfort in the recitation of the Kaddish.

Jack's next words to the congregation revealed which story he embraced:

> Through introspection I visit Nicholas and I can find beauty in his smile. I was fortunate to have spent incredible time with my son in the seven and a half years God bestowed upon us. I am grateful I did not miss the opportunity I did have. If I were given the choice to never have known Nicholas or to have known Nicholas at the price of suffering and losing him, the choice would be simple. I am forever thankful for being Nicholas's father. I understand he is no longer in my stewardship; he is in God's hands. I have let him go.

Jack had retold the story of Beruriah and Rabbi Meir.

Aggadah is the language of Jewish faith; stories about real human situations are an integral part of its theological discourse. Through a variety of stories our rabbinic sages and seers helped themselves to affirm the meaning of life even in the midst of anguish and undeserved suffering. There are no ready-made answers, but the stories do indicate a process for healing. As a teacher of religious faith, I have marveled at the wisdom of those sages and storytellers. They offer us multiple narratives that reflect the individual temperament and religious imagination of their authors. But for all its flexibility, *Aggadah* gives us one clear ground rule: Find within these stories a way to reaffirm your faith. Doubt and despair may not be given the last word in the story of our lives.

Chapter 2

What Kind of Life Is This Anyway?

And God saw all that He had made, and found it very good.
—Genesis 1:31

THE CAB DRIVER WHO took us to the airport shared this tale of woe. He had left his car on the street in front of his apartment building. A hit-and-run driver sideswiped it, causing considerable damage. He had no collision insurance. So our cab driver fumed at an unidentifiable perpetrator and shared with us this summary judgment on life, "What's the use? The moment you think you've handled one thing you're bashed by another."

My wife and I could have challenged him to place his present trouble on the scale with our own. We had just visited my mother-in-law, who, after weeks in the ICU, developed additional complications that left us wondering whether to pray for a miraculous healing or her final release. We could have said, "Be grateful, it's only a car." In the heat of his anger, however, the driver needed our sympathetic ear.

It seemed to us that our cab driver was expressing his view on more than one frustrating incident, that even before this episode he had arrived at a dour view of his lot and of life itself. Perhaps today's episode of bad luck was just the latest in a series of misfortunes. If we had asked him, "So, what kind of life is this anyway?" he might well have responded, "Life stinks!"

Some tragedies are greater than normal setbacks and stay with us for a long time. One such story is of a former policeman and fireman who owns a restaurant in Far Rockaway, New York—a small community across the bay from Manhattan. On the day of the terrorist attack on the World Trade Center, the restaurant owner lost his son who worked in one of the towers. The owner personally knew ninety people who were killed in that disaster, most of them firemen and policemen, many of them his neighbors and customers.

After two months of bitter tears and grieving, the man was traumatized by a fresh disaster. A large airliner crashed into his neighborhood, killing all on board, destroying the homes of his neighbors, and claiming the lives of six more people from his town. Even those of us who were not directly touched by the events of September 11 feel depressed by the state of the world and anxious about the dangers and uncertainty of life. Where do we find the strength to go on in times like these?

My answer to the question—What kind of life is this anyway?—is shaped by the stories of the Jewish spiritual tradition. These stories do not offer me a single answer to life's deepest questions but they do give me a landscape on which to pursue my quest for faith.

Both Judaism and Christianity derive their orientation from the creation story in the early pages of Genesis. We read, "When God began to create heaven and earth—the earth being unformed and void, with darkness over the surface of the deep and a wind from God sweeping over the water—God said, 'Let there be light'; and there was light. God saw that the light was good" (Genesis 1:1-4).

The Hebrew Bible proclaims that God the Creator infused form on an earth that was wild and waste. God created order out of chaos—light out of the darkness. This primordial light is the symbol of a world infused with value and meaning. Repeatedly God says of each phase of the creative process, "And it was good." After human life had appeared God says, "And it was very good." The Torah insists that the world into which we have been thrust is *cosmos,* not chaos. There is an order to the universe God created. Rabbi Adin Steinsaltz calls this claim "a firm belief . . . that there is some sense in things."[1]

But anyone who reads the Bible knows that almost at once the assertion of life's goodness and meaning becomes problematic. Throughout the book of Genesis we find dysfunctional families, murder, flood, war—and the reality of undeserved suffering. And what about the undeserved suffering and rampant evil in our time?

We have all seen times of trouble, both individually and collectively. So did the ancient rabbis who inherited the creation story with its declaration of life's goodness. They knew the ravages of war, the bitterness of exile, as well as the suffering of the innocent. Rabbi Yannai, a third century sage who lived at the time of the Roman occupation of Judea concluded, "It is not in our power to explain the prosperity of the wicked or the afflictions of the righteous."[2] And yet, they rejected the conclusion that life has no meaning. They insisted that God's creation is good and that there is a transcendent value and purpose to our lives. How did they do it?

Some rabbis concluded that life is meaningful because what appears evil may actually turn out for the best. To support this view, they cited the biblical Joseph story. Joseph's brothers, deeply resentful of his favored status in their father Jacob's eyes, placed him in a pit in the wilderness and then sold him to a caravan of slave traders bound for Egypt. The brothers fully expected never to see their brother again, and as far as they were concerned, good riddance.

In Egypt the young Joseph rose to a high position in Pharaoh's court. During famine in the land of Canaan, the brothers were forced to go to Egypt to purchase grain. There they encountered Joseph, now Egypt's food czar. At first Joseph concealed his identity. He tested the brothers. When he finally revealed himself to them they were terrified. Joseph calmed them by asserting, "Now, do not be distressed or reproach yourselves because you sold me hither; it was to save life that God sent me ahead of you . . . and to save your lives in an extraordinary deliverance" (Genesis 45:5-7). Joseph contended that if his brothers had not sold him to Egypt, he would not be in a position to save them and their father.

This perspective, that what appears evil may turn out to be good, finds its extreme expression in talmudic stories about Nahum Gamzo. Whatever distress befell him, he would always say, "*Gam zo le-tovah,*" meaning "This too is for the best." Hence his nickname "Gamzo." In one tale, the sages of Israel dispatched Nahum to deliver a gift of gold and silver to the Roman emperor. On his way to the palace, Nahum spent the night at an inn. Unbeknownst to him, robbers stole the treasure in his saddlebags and filled those bags with earth. Unaware of what had happened to his treasure, Nahum arrived at Caesar's palace and presented his gift. When the emperor found the bags were full of earth, he issued orders for Nahum's execution.

At that moment the prophet Elijah appeared, disguised as one of Caesar's senators, and convinced the emperor that what appeared to be earth in those saddlebags was actually a powerful substance to confound Caesar's enemies and force them to surrender. Caesar demanded to test the substance in battle. His army flung the earth at the enemy and succeeded in conquering them. The delighted Caesar rewarded Nahum, still in custody, by filling his chest with precious stones and pearls and sending him home in honor. Whereupon Nahum proclaimed, "This too is for the best."[3]

While we may regard the Nahum story as a miraculous fable, the perspective it represents sustained many Jewish believers across the centuries. This view essentially declares that all that happens must ultimately be consistent with God's beneficent plan. Therefore, when troubles engulf us we must acknowledge our limited understanding and trust in our Creator. We hope that in time we, too, will understand and discover that "everything is for the best."

At least some of the time, our experience seems to support this view of life. We have all sought something that we were denied. At the time, we may have felt considerable grief, but years later it became evident that the way things worked out was for the best. Many years ago, I was one of two candidates for the presidency of the Hebrew Union College. The other candidate was chosen. At the time I did some grieving, but in retrospect it was a blessing both for me and for the College. By temperament and interests I was really best suited to spend my life as a congregational rabbi, and I now know it.

I have known individuals who were crestfallen when they lost their jobs. Some decided to go into business for themselves and became very successful. Realizing that they might not otherwise have ever taken this step, they now are able to say that, "getting fired was the best thing that ever happened to me." Some persons may grieve over a lover who jilted them only to discover much later that the person they later married was better suited for them.

In retrospect, there are occasions in all our lives when we would say, "This too is for the best." Yet I seriously doubt any of us could fully rest our faith on such a foundation. Too much pain and suffering in this world resists being construed as a blessing in disguise. When it comes to real grief and loss, it seems almost a sacrilege to say "everything is for the best."

Another tale about Nahum of Gamzo is darker and more intriguing. Nahum is on the road taking provisions of food to his father-in-law when he meets a beggar who asks for water to drink. Nahum tells him, "Wait till I unload the asses." Meanwhile, the beggar dies. Nahum is so remorseful that he asks to be inflicted with the beggar's helplessness and becomes blind and crippled. Finding him in this sorry state, his rabbinic colleagues declare, "Woe that we found you like this!" but Nahum responds, "Woe had you not found me like this!"[4] What could he mean by this? Some say Nahum learned the heart of the helpless through his affliction, which allowed him to become a great sage.

To us moderns, this view is extremely disturbing. It is not clear that suffering necessarily improves anyone. Many people claim that they have grown in insight and wisdom through suffering, but it is unlikely that any would have chosen their misfortunes as Nahum had.

A second view of evil presented by the rabbinic sages takes a cue from Genesis 47:7-10. "Joseph then brought his father Jacob and presented him to Pharaoh. . . . Pharaoh asked Jacob, 'How many are the years of your life?' And Jacob answered Pharaoh, '. . . Few and hard have been the years of my life, nor do they come up to the life spans of my fathers during their sojourns.' "

A rabbinic commentary elaborates: "You ask how many years I have *lived*. I have not *lived*. The years I have had have not been a life—but almost a living death, so much have I suffered, and so many bitter experiences have I had. . . . If you can comprehend my grief, you will understand why I appear so very old."[5]

No doubt the rabbis were referring to Jacob's years of exile and flight from his brother Esau's vengeful wrath, the years of indentured labor for his father-in-law Laban, the death of his beloved wife Rachel in childbirth, the rape of his daughter Dinah, and Jacob's grief during the years he feared Joseph was dead.

Surely the rabbis who seized upon Jacob's travails (and knew their own) could not claim that everything in life turns out for the best. How then did they square this grim view of their life, and of Jacob's, with faith in the goodness of creation and the meaning of existence? They did so by their belief in a world beyond this earthly life.

The rabbis affirmed that God's creation is good because the creation includes this world and "the World-to-Come." The "World-to-Come" has two meanings; it may refer to the Messianic Age at the end of history when this hapless world will be totally redeemed and God's dream of justice, love, and peace will be fulfilled. Or it may refer to the world beyond our mortal span where the individual soul will be reunited with the Soul of souls and the injustices and ambiguities of this world will be finally resolved. This grim view of earthly life is reminiscent of a traditional dirge I remember from childhood, "In this world, sorrow and sighing / In the World-to-Come, a Sabbath of perfect peace."

This view is not so far from us, even for those who do not believe in an afterlife or a perfectly redeemed world. When we think about the innocent victims of the Holocaust, whose lives were cut short so brutally, and about the Nazi perpetrators, many of whom finished their lives in peace and tranquillity, we can't help but hope for a God who will see to justice in some form beyond our grasp. It is a human hope—as well as a biblical promise—that God cares about justice. We hope for justice when the righting of wrongs is beyond our means.

In life, persons who perform heroic deeds may suffer terribly and even pay the supreme price for their nobility. And some persons are so monstrously evil that no human punishment, including the death penalty, is commensurate with the deed. Such realities have stirred the hope, sometimes ripening into faith, that by God's justice the postmortal destiny of an Adolf Hitler is not the same as the postmortal destiny of Mother Teresa.

I suspect few if any of us troubled souls would be content with only the consolation of eternal life in a world beyond this earth. Fortunately, there is a third way that both acknowledges the darker side of existence and yet affirms the goodness of this life. This view simply acknowledges the existence of both good and evil as part of life and accepts the whole with gratitude.

We see this view expressed in the traditional Jewish wedding ceremony. When bride and groom stand under the *chuppah* (bridal canopy) blessings are recited that include the following, "We praise You, Adonai our God, Ruler of the universe, Creator of joy and gladness, man and woman, love and kinship, peace and friendship. . . . We praise You, our God, who causes husband and wife to rejoice together."[6]

Bride and groom then share a cup of sweet wine—symbol of the joy of creation. But the ceremony also includes the presentation of a *ketubah*—a marriage contract, duly signed and witnessed, that obligates the groom to treat his wife with respect. In its traditional form, the *ketubah* suggests that the joy of love is not enough to protect the bride from the dark contingencies of this world. She needs a legal contract.

At the end of the ceremony, a glass is broken. One popular interpretation is that even at a time of peak joy, we must remember the tragedy of the Temple's destruction and the fall of Jerusalem. I haven't yet met a bride and groom who can think of the Temple's destruction at such a time, but all in attendance are well aware of life's double-edged nature. They may be thinking of their own disappointed hopes and trials. They will nod knowingly when I remind bride and groom that "we wish for you a life of perfect happiness, unalloyed with trial and trouble, but we know as you know that every life is touched by sorrow as well as joy, by defeat as well as triumph."

Life is both a cup of sweet wine and a broken glass. Sometimes we ourselves break the glass and are the makers of the troubles that engulf us. Sometimes we are the victims of another's irresponsible acts, insensitivities, or indifference. Sometimes we experience a brokenness that is part of the natural course of the physical world, including illness or adversity. Some trouble seems to be the price we pay for life's goodness. Love is wonderful, but to love is to sacrifice and suffer for and with those we love. And no one can hurt us more than the ones to whom we are bound in love.

What then does it mean to declare life is good? It does not mean there is no evil or that everything happens for the best. Neither does it mean that we must mortgage our faith in life's goodness to the anticipation of a Messianic Age or the promise of bliss in the World-to-Come. This view of life is foreshadowed in the words of an ancient sage, "It is incumbent on a person to praise God for the evil as for the good." I take this to mean that we must accept life on God's terms and proclaim that the total package that is our life, with its joy and pain intertwined, is worth the price—that our given life, this earthly life, has meaning and value.

The declaration that life is good *may* be affirmed at times because of what we have experienced; it must be affirmed at times in spite of our experience. The cup of joy and the broken glass declare that life's hurts are real, as real as the joy.

Not all that happens in the world may happen as God wants it. Darkness and tears of sadness are very much a part of our lives and, as it were, of God's as well. But God is present even in the darkness, and a source of strength in our darkest moments.

To be sure, some persons do seem to have been dealt a much harsher fate than others. While some must endure chronic ill health, economic adversity, or the wounds of poor family relationships, others seem blessed with a relatively carefree existence. Still, my counseling experience suggests that the circumstances of our lives are not a reliable predictor of life attitudes. Some persons with an ostensibly easy life have a more morose outlook than those who have been severely buffeted by adversity.

Whether we affirm that life is or is not worth the price remains essentially an act of faith. When it comes to such questions, life is not a problem to solve but a mystery to embrace. Despite their experiences with adversity and disappointment, many have never surrendered their faith in God or their belief that life has meaning.

Physician and psychotherapist Rachel Naomi Remen writes of visiting her Orthodox grandfather late Friday afternoons when she was only five years old. Because his wife had died, each week her grandfather would light and bless the Sabbath candles himself. He would then give Rachel a tiny cup with a thimbleful of sweet wine. After the appropriate blessings he would invite her to say "*L'haim*," and to drink the wine. Rachel once asked him, "What does it mean to say '*L'haim*'?" He translated, "To life!" When she still seemed puzzled by this toast to life, her grandfather explained: "No matter what difficulty life brings, no matter how hard or painful or unfair life is, life is holy and worthy of celebration."[7] In other words, life is good, because life itself is a blessing.

This vignette from childhood is included in her memoir, *My Grandfather's Blessings.* In the future Rachel would be severely challenged by her grandfather's words. Since adolescence Rachel has suffered with Crohn's disease. The physician who first made the diagnosis told her she would not live to the age of forty. She is now in her mid-sixties.

Sometime ago my friend Lyon Cohen sent me a news clipping about Jim Valvano, the successful college basketball coach and TV sportscaster. When Valvano received the chilling medical report that his days were numbered, he continued to work at ESPN as long as he could. Then shortly before his death he made a public statement few would have expected from him a decade earlier, "We should do this everyday of our lives. Number one is laugh. You should laugh every day. Number two is think. You should spend some time in thought. And number three is, you should have your emotions moved to tears, could be happiness or joy. . . . If you laugh, you think, and you cry, that's a full day."[8]

Lyon sent me that Valvano clipping because it obviously touched him. He highlighted Valvano's last public statement in yellow. The clipping moved me even more deeply because of what I know about its sender. Lyon lived on the edge. Over the years he had a series of very serious brain surgeries and long convalescences with no promise of total cure. In the face of these struggles Lyon enjoyed life, love, good food, sports, and grandchildren. As an accountant, he fulfilled his responsibilities to his clients. He related to his family with the intensity and appreciation of one who knew that life has a darker side, that our days are finite, and that memories of joy and love live on.

Lyon Cohen died some years ago. He lived at least a dozen years beyond his neurosurgeon's projections. We who loved him mourned his loss, but in taking the measure of his years we beheld, not a hapless victim of the world's unfairness, but a man of great courage who, after each of his five brain surgeries in eighteen years, persistently made a toast—*L'haim*, to life!

I imagine there were times when Lyon could not look at the package of life and accept it, much less call it good. Our greatest sages and other persons of faith also had those moments. But Lyon eloquently embodied for me this acceptance of life on its own terms. He believed, "You have to play the hand you're dealt." He acknowledged that life is both a cup of sweet wine and a broken glass, and most of the time Lyon affirmed that life was worth its price.

If life's circumstances are not an adequate predictor of our attitudes, what then shapes our life perspective? Clearly, the verdict "life stinks" takes us nowhere, yet some of us find it impossible to accept life as worth its price. When I reread the ancient rabbis, I wonder, is it because we have so much more to cope with than our ancestors? Or is it because we have lost their sense of living in the presence of God? If so, can we allow ourselves the option of religious faith? To that question we next turn.

Chapter 3

Confronting the Obstacles to Faith

The LORD alone is God in heaven above and on earth below; there is no other. —Deuteronomy 4:39

MANY OF THE TRIALS our ancestors endured are ours as well, but one thing may have changed. The biblical Jacob knew that he lived in the presence of God. God was his ultimate helper in coping with life's darker side. The psalmists spoke of God as the healer of broken hearts and the binder of their wounds (Psalm 147:3). Rabbi Israel, the Baal Shem Tov, Master of the Good Name, told Rabbi Pinhas, "We are not alone."

For many a child of modernity, God may seem at best the absentee landlord of the universe. We may pay lip service to institutional piety or belong to a synagogue or church, and still not experience God as truly present in our lives. Some of us regard simple piety as only for unsophisticated souls. We may concede that religion promotes morality and religious ritual has some social value in marking the milestones of the life cycle, but many find it difficult to embrace the fundamental premise of classic Western religion: that there is a God who created us, who cares for us, and who guides and helps us on our earthly journey.

It is easy to dismiss the claims of religion in a postmodern age. Modern men and women, we believe, solve problems with science and technology, not prayer. The truths we live by are no longer revealed in commandments and sacred stories but need to be proved in a laboratory or demonstrated by logical argument. In the past we might have turned to a rabbi or priest for guidance but now we are more apt to seek the counsel of a physician or psychotherapist. In a time of illness, one of my congregants confessed, "I'm not sure I know how to pray. God and I are not on speaking terms."

Some who deny themselves the religious option may protest, "How can I believe in God when there is so much undeserved suffering in the world?" But we also know that in the darker times of life we wish we could draw nearer to a comforting God, "the healer of broken hearts and the binder of their wounds." The great Russian writer Leo Tolstoy insisted that, whatever our formal declaration, each of us needs to live by a faith in the ultimate significance of our life. Faith gives to personal life that ultimate meaning that is not destroyed even by suffering or death.

How do we grasp the spirituality that appears so peculiarly underdeveloped among many of us? Spirituality finds its deepest expression in our connectedness to an ultimate reality both within and beyond ourselves. Hebrew Scripture refers to God by many names: *Adonai* (Master, Lord), *Makom* (the Place), *Tzur* (Rock), *Shekhinah* (Divine Presence).

In the Hebrew Bible, four Hebrew letters that may be represented in English as *Y-H-W-H* signify the name of God. The letters appear related to the Hebrew verb that means "to be." This four-letter name could not be pronounced by anyone except the high priest on Yom Kippur, the Day of Atonement, when he entered the Holy of Holies of the ancient Temple in Jerusalem. To this day when we confront the letters *Y-H-W-H*, as we study Torah or pray, we do not utter them. Instead, we substitute the word *Adonai,* which simply means "the Lord." There is a reason we do not speak the name of God aloud.

God is the Nameless One. To name something is part of the human quest for complete understanding and control. Adam named the animals in the garden of Eden as a way of gaining mastery over them. We name a disease as part of our effort to conquer it. The real God is beyond being fully named or understood or controlled by human beings. God remains irreducibly *Y-H-W-H,* the infinite, mysterious Source of being.

The Bible tells the story of this infinite and mysterious God who seeks a relationship and even a covenant with mortal human beings. This connection to the divine endows human life with meaning. The God to whom we are connected is the Source of Being, who reveals the way we are intended to live, as embodied in the terms of the covenant, and is present both in our lives and in history as helper and redeemer.

Now as in the past, what distinguishes the believer from nonbeliever is the perspective that each brings to the world. Faith is a way of perceiving the world. An ancient psalmist looked up at the starry sky and declared, "The heavens declare the glory of God, / and the sky proclaims His handiwork" (19:1). Closer to our time, science fiction writer H. G. Wells saw a panoply of stars and said it reminded him of nothing more than a pattern of wallpaper in a railroad station.

I visit a hospital room where parents are holding and admiring their newborn child together for the first time. The mother asks me, "Who do you think he looks like, Rabbi?" The father jokes, "Shall we start saving for college? This is it for us, Rabbi. We can't afford more."

I enter another room on the maternity floor and find a mother holding her newly born daughter. Her eyes well up with tears, "What a miracle, Rabbi." These words are the perfect segue to the prayer we recite together, "Praised are You, O God, Ruler of the universe, who has kept us in life, sustained us, and enabled us to experience this moment."

The entry of a newborn child into our world may be seen simply as the natural outcome when mother and father engage in sexual intimacy at a ripe time. But a child's birth may also be viewed as one of God's wondrous gifts.

Many moderns have approached such birth scenes in a secular rather than religious way because of the mind-set that shapes their world. They assume that our ancestors prayed to God for a child because they did not understand the science of reproduction and fertility—and certainly did not have recourse to fertility drugs and in vitro procedures. They may even see religion as a primitive form of science. Now, they assert, we have better forms of explanation.

Such a view assumes that if you view life religiously, you are denying the truth claims of science. Actually, the scientific and religious perspectives are complementary, not mutually exclusive. Even science and medicine are less about hard facts than the art of interpreting data. Faith is another way of interpreting reality.

I may attend a concert and focus attention on Itzhak Perlman as he plays the Brahm's Violin Concerto. On a sheer physical level, I am experiencing the sound produced by pulling a stick strung with horsehair over a stick strung with catgut. But I may also experience the awesome artistry of the violinist and the mysterious transforming power of the music as God's gift. We may rationally embrace both perspectives. Even so, the birth of a baby is a biological phenomenon, but the event may also be received as a gift from the Source of all being.

Martin Buber, the twentieth-century Jewish thinker, applied this dual perspective to the biblical story of Israel's deliverance at the Red Sea. He maintained that the Exodus story rests on a kernel of history embellished by legend. The book of Exodus tells us that the Israelites were able to cross a body of water that later proved impassable by the pursuing Egyptians. Buber assumes that if we knew all there was to know about that event, we could conceivably describe it as an entirely natural process. Perhaps the water was not very deep to begin with and a combination of changing tide and wind patterns made it passable for the Israelites, but later impassable for the Egyptian chariots. According to Buber, the miracle did not consist of a violation of the laws of nature but rather in the way those natural elements combined precisely at the moment when the Israelites needed them to make their escape. The miracle consisted of the Israelites seeing within a natural process a sign of God's decisive redeeming power. A nonbeliever present at that event might have concluded otherwise. Whether or not an event is a miracle depends, to some extent, on the eye of the beholder.

Actually, from ancient times through the present, belief in God's presence has never been the result of a blatantly obvious divine appearance. Religious faith has always depended on the way we interpret and perceive the events in our world. Even in ancient times, some people did not view the heavens as a sign of God's power and creative majesty. The psalmist takes note of such people in saying, "How great are Your works, O LORD, / how very subtle Your designs! / A brutish man cannot know, / a fool cannot understand this" (Psalm 92:6-7). God was then and remains to this day an elusive presence. The Holy One does not force the divine self upon us with spectacular, preternatural displays. Faith is demanding because the presence of God is often subtle.

Another obstacle to faith is the belief that the stories of the Bible must be taken as literal truth or not at all. Many of us cannot believe that six hundred thousand men stood at Sinai (not counting the wives and children). Such a mass of people would have extended from the Sinai wilderness all the way to the promised land! We may also doubt that the plagues took place exactly as described.

Every year around Passover time, there is a spate of articles questioning whether the exodus ever took place. In addition, archaeologists who have extensively excavated the region find virtually no evidence of Israelite slaves in Egypt or an exodus. The Stele of Merneptah, one of the few surviving relics of the thirteenth century B.C.E., simply mentions "Israel" in a long list of peoples defeated by Egypt. On the other hand, there is very little archaeological evidence for anything in the thirteenth century B.C.E., and escaping slaves did not leave monuments! All we have is an oral history that attests to a powerful collective experience.

Do such controversies put my own faith in question? Not at all, because for me sacred narratives like the exodus story were never intended to be strictly historical accounts. These stories are not validated by scientific experiments or archaeological expeditions. Their truth is derived from the meaning and healing they give to those who hear and are shaped by them. To people of faith, the exodus story offers the deepest understanding of the human experience in history.

Over the centuries, when the Roman Emperor Hadrian, or the Spanish inquisitor Torquemada, or Hitler, or Stalin oppressed the Jewish people, these tyrants were seen as successors to the prototypical oppressor, Pharaoh. The story of the Israelites' deliverance from Egypt, retold annually at the Passover Seder, affirms the faith that God—not Pharaoh—will have the last word in history. And indeed, the survival of the Jewish people through some of these periods has been no less than miraculous.

The exodus story has also helped other peoples understand their history and yearnings. It has inspired many freedom movements across the centuries including the War of Independence of the original American colonies. The Founding Fathers actually proposed a scene depicting the biblical exodus as a seal for the new nation. In our own time, the African American struggle for Civil Rights found in the biblical saga of God's deliverance an inspiration for believing that "we shall overcome." Centuries earlier, black slaves sang the spiritual "Go Down, Moses," which retells the exodus story and includes the battle cry for freedom, "Let my people go!"

When we confront "bondage" in our personal lives, the exodus narrative may also ground our hopes for deliverance. I met Jenny when she came to talk to me about her search for spirituality and a stronger relation to God. Jenny grew up in a home with a tyrannical and abusive father and a passively submissive mother. With the help of a therapist and a deeply understanding husband, Jenny has come a long way in her own liberation, but she still feels the emotional scarring from those years of abuse and struggles with bouts of low self-esteem.

Jenny told me of her difficulty trusting and drawing near to a God who is so powerful, and at times, punitive. I told her there are many facets to the God described in the Bible and Talmud. These are, after all, human attempts to grasp the Ultimate Mystery. Based on our own experience and reading of religious texts, we can accept or reject certain depictions of the divine nature.

When we turned to the exodus story, Jenny was at first bothered by what she called the "power thing." She admitted she had trouble relating to powerful authority figures, whether human or divine. As we probed further, she suddenly realized that story pits a powerful, oppressive king (who thought he was divine) against a God who champions the Israelites' right to be free. She came to see the story as an affirmation that God's power and graciousness are on the side of the oppressed. One of the primary elements of faith embedded in the exodus story is that God helps us in our battles against oppressors, and that to God—not the tyrant, and not the abusing parent—belongs the final victory. That insight ripened into a faith that enabled Jenny to deepen her relationship to God. She felt newly empowered in her continuing struggle to cast off vestiges of her difficult childhood.

One of the great struggles of those who have endured abusive relationships is to keep themselves from perpetrating that abuse in relation to their own children. As the mother of two young sons, Jenny was not unmindful of that danger. She noted with deep appreciation that the God who freed Israel from bondage commands the people not to perpetuate the cycle of oppression and injustice. In the words of the commandment, God says, "You shall not oppress a stranger, for you know the feelings of the stranger, having yourselves been strangers in the land of Egypt" (Exodus 23:9). The God who helps us win our freedom from oppression can also help us overcome the inclination to be an oppressor.

Why do we believe that acts that brutalize or demean other human beings are wrong? Some may argue that such moral indignation is simply the result of cultural conditioning or evolution. After all, compassion for the helpless has survival value; otherwise, society would become a jungle. But to persons of faith, the passion for justice and the revulsion at the exploitation of the weak are rooted in a teaching that is divinely inspired. God commands, "You shall not oppress the stranger . . . having yourselves been strangers in the land of Egypt" (Exodus 23:9).

The leading character in Saul Bellow's novel *Mr. Sammler's Planet* powerfully expresses the transcendent standard by which we judge the integrity of our lives. Sammler, an elderly survivor of the Holocaust, stands at the grave of his nephew-benefactor and says, "Remember, God, the soul of Elya Gruner. . . . At his best this man was . . . aware that he must meet, and he did meet . . . the terms of his contract. The terms which, in his inmost heart, each man knows. As I know mine. . . . For that is the truth of it—that we all know, God, that we know, that we know, we know."[1]

I suspect there are intimations of God as creator, redeemer, and lawgiver in all our lives, but still many people are reluctant to see their own lives and experiences in religious terms. They have not been drawn to take the faith option. Their evident discomfort with spirituality is a reflection of our secular age.

A final obstacle to faith is the image of religion as a divisive and even a destructive force. Looking at the sorry state of the world today, it is easy to hold religion responsible for many of the evils we see—intolerance, fanaticism, conflict, and hatred. Who needs religion if it creates differences among people? Although religion has played an important role in culture, it has all too often been put to use for political ends. Faith has acquired a bad name when we think of the excesses of fanaticism and intolerance—the Crusades, the Inquisition, and in our day, the terrorists waging "holy war." Few of us would want to surrender our ability to think independently or to submit to brainwashing for someone else's ends. Yet can we surrender our yearning for personal meaning and connection to God? The pursuit of faith is about as personal as any quest could be, and we cannot afford to let its distortions by religious extremists ruin that option for us. Faith is an unquenchable human need—and religious teachings, at their best, can help us in our quest for the things we value most.

How comfortable are we moderns living without a spiritual component in our lives? Do we care about our connection to God? I would suggest that many of us are not as comfortable as we might have been thirty, forty, or fifty years ago.

There was indeed a time when the mark of enlightenment in intellectual circles meant a certain degree of skepticism and indifference to religion. While many may remain uneasy with "God talk," I detect much more openness among most people I encounter to spiritual concerns, and many wish they could draw sustenance from a sustaining faith.

When I was a student at Harvard in the early 1950s, religious discourse was not intellectually fashionable among students or faculty. You kept any religious impulses pretty much to yourself as a "closet believer." It took some courage to proclaim religious interests. The Harvard Divinity School was a stepchild in the university family. Little academic attention was given the symbols and beliefs of the great historical religions, except in the context of a sociology or anthropology course.

Today at Harvard and virtually all the elite campuses, including Rice University where I taught for over two decades, religious studies have earned great respectability. Many of the courses are well attended and the students bring to class not only an intellectual curiosity but also a personal quest to explore their relationship to the sacred.

Why this new openness to religion in the academic world? There has been a cultural shift. Some have spoken of a transition from the modern to the postmodern age. In the modern world, secular politics once promised to create the ideal society. Political ideologies became the focus of ultimate hope for millions. Believers were encouraged to place their faith, not in God, but in political messianism. Communism is a classic case of a substitute religion that promised a classless society but produced instead a brutal totalitarian state. By the 1950s, many former Communists felt betrayed by, as a book title at the time called it, "the god that failed."

What is true of our changing attitude to politics also applies to the realm of technology and science. It is easy to understand how we came to invest nuclear reactors, space shuttles, and superconductors with the awe that our pre-modern ancestors reserved for the forces of nature and for God. But in worshiping the works of our own hands, we are actually worshiping ourselves.

Several stories from the Talmud tell about the Roman Emperor Hadrian who was so impressed by his own power that he sought to have himself proclaimed a deity. When Hadrian returned from his latest conquest and demanded to be deified by his court philosophers, one rejected that claim by reminding the emperor that his power was less than divine. To return a lost vessel to shore, Hadrian had to dispatch other vessels to tow it in, whereas God could activate the winds! On that basis, the philosopher debunked the emperor's claims to divinity, "If you have no control over the winds, how can you declare yourself God?"[2]

How far we have come since that tale was first told. So much power lies in our hands today! In our age of high technology, the vessel might be a nuclear-powered space ship returned to earth by pulling a switch. At its best, the power of technology is awesome and beautiful. Amazing diagnostic machines and bold surgeries such as heart bypasses have dramatically lengthened the human life span. Advanced technologies allow us to anticipate and prepare for many of nature's destructive rampages, saving thousands of lives. And biogenetic research promises so much for the future.

No wonder many of technology's most ardent advocates believe that "what we can't do today, we will do tomorrow." We can bend the environment to our needs. But in the latter half of the twentieth century, we have been assaulted by a new sense of limits. We realize that we have the power to build as well as to destroy and we do not always have the wisdom to know the difference. We see that our dominion over nature has threatened us with ecological disaster. Already in ancient times a rabbi imagined God saying to Adam in the garden of Eden, "Behold all which I have created is for your benefit but beware lest you despoil and destroy my world, for if you do, there is no one to repair it after you."[3]

Now as we contemplate the destruction of the ozone layer and the deleterious effect of pollution on our health we find new urgency in that ancient admonition. We must take more seriously the biblical notion that we are responsible stewards of the garden of life. As biologist Garret Hardin has written, "The essentially religious feeling of subserviency to a power greater than ourselves comes hard to us clever people. But by our intelligence we are now beginning to make out the limits to our cleverness. . . . We are experiencing a return to a religious orientation toward the world."[4]

What is true for the environment is also true for death itself. Ever since the garden of Eden, human beings have wanted to outwit the angel of death. In our time we have made great strides against infant mortality and aging, and these are regarded as only the tip of the technological iceberg. Death itself has become for some a technological problem in need of solution. But there has been a discernible change. We rarely hear of people freezing their bodies until the mystery of death is solved. Although we want to defer the day of death as long as there is some quality to our life, we know, as did our ancestors, that death is part of life. We now seek to discern the difference between prolonging life and only prolonging dying, and we want to die with dignity. In a postmodern age, the goddess technology has lost some of her aura.

Science itself is no longer seen as the ultimate answer to our problems. Many of the truths we live by do not submit to a laboratory test. Even scientists at work must deal with unprovable assumptions, invisible entities, and evolving ideas about a cosmos that eludes their grasp. We now realize that science and technology raise but do not answer many of the most important questions of life, such as "Who am I?" "How shall I live my life?" "What can I hope for?"

In a sense, we are all believers. We seek meaning in our existence by our beliefs and loyalties to things, ideas, persons. It is good to cherish these loyalties and values, as long as they do not keep us from connecting to the One who alone invests our life with its ultimate significance. Our biblical ancestors abhorred idolatry because they realized that anything worshiped in place of the unknowable and nameless God can lead to evil. Sooner or later we too discover that there is no god but God.

The journey to a recovery of faith may not be simple. Even those who readily acknowledge the failure of modernity's gods are still uncomfortable with the idea of trusting in God and unsure of what that means. They wish they could embrace the healing power and consolations of religion, but they feel that intellectual honesty requires agnosticism at best. Fortunately, the changed cultural climate has encouraged even the skeptics among us to acknowledge religious yearnings and explore the possible role of faith in our lives. The universe is a lonely place without it.

Chapter 4

Recovering Faith—
A Guide to a Deeper Spirituality

The LORD is near to all who call Him . . . with sincerity.
—Psalm 145

IN A *NEW YORKER* piece titled "The Art of Failing," journalist James Atlas writes of an interview with an old friend, Dean Valentine, who had "made it big" as a top executive in the Disney Television empire. When Atlas called to set up the interview, his friend confessed, "I'm shocked that success has meant so little to me. . . . I'm still very driven. I want to do well. And success has helped me with my insecurity. But—I know this sounds weird—it seems increasingly irrelevant. It never feels real from the inside."[1] Many circumstances in our lives may create a particularly ripe moment for thinking about faith. One such moment arises when our customary strategies for living break down. Another is when even the good stuff suddenly appears insufficient to make our lives feel whole.

Saul Bellow's protagonist in *Henderson the Rain King* is a fifty-five-year-old Connecticut Yankee with a wife and children, a good job, and social respectability. Nevertheless, he wakes up one night and hears his soul crying out "I want, I want, I want!"[2] At certain times in life, such hungers of the soul penetrate our defenses. Although most of us would agree with the statement, "If you've got your health, you've got it all," we may still feel that a lifestyle devoted to dieting, jogging, and working out does not in itself add up to a fully authentic life. We may be among those fortunate ones who enjoy their work and have attained success, yet the soul signals this too is not enough. Or we may be like the beautiful middle-aged woman I encountered who suddenly discovered that fund-raising for good causes at high profile benefits and seeing her name and photograph frequently in the society pages were not enough to give her that sense of meaning we all crave.

More commonly, we open a window to faith when the threat of life's darker side assaults us. To be suddenly confronted by the prospect of serious surgery can open the mind and heart to faith. A congregant who received two benign reports from a pathology lab exclaimed to me, "Rabbi, I have just dodged two bullets and it has made me think about lots of things for the first time."

At times like these, we don't always know where to turn. Carol, a wife and mother of two young adults, is also a leader of art tours to fine museums and galleries all over the world. A visit to the doctor revealed that Carol needed to undergo very risky surgery for the removal of a rare tumor lodged near her brain. She and her husband had decided to travel to a distant medical center that specialized in this surgery and claimed to have the highest success rate. Before they left, I visited with them at their home. Carol is a sophisticated, cultured woman, who is proud of her Jewish heritage. We spent more than an hour during which I gave her a small book of prayers to say before surgery, during recovery, and for the difficult postoperative days. I shared my conviction that the healing power within and beyond us can be enhanced when we acknowledge our neediness. I encouraged her to recite those prayers and some of her own.

Her husband David called me as soon as he had received a favorable report from the surgeon. He told me that the time we spent preparing Carol for surgery was very important for both of them. Carol later thanked me herself and confided to a friend that she was surprised to discover the comfort and healing she derived from saying those prayers.

Any life experience that underscores our essential vulnerability and lack of full control may open us to the spiritual side of our nature. Eight years ago, my wife and I radically remodeled our home. It became the comfortable space we hoped would be there for us through our retirement years. One stormy night shattered those expectations. Lightning struck and ignited a fire that destroyed our home. We were physically spared, but we lost many of our possessions including my library of over seven hundred treasured books.

Fortunately for me, the larger part of my library was at the Temple. But those books I kept at home were trusted companions. I knew where each was on the shelves and I had made many personal annotations in most of them. I could count on them for my reading pleasure and as a resource for preaching. Being surrounded by those familiar books always comforted me. A few days after the fire, we rented a temporary apartment and basic furnishings. I now required only one small bookcase and it was largely empty. When my wife Joan saw it, she wept.

At the time I wrote about the experience in *The Houston Chronicle,* "When I am asked where do Joan and I plan to make our permanent residence, I mentally place the word permanent in quotation marks. As the poet Wallace Stevens wrote: 'We live in a place that is not our own.' Our real home is the frail, vulnerable, *sukkah* (booth) which Hebrew Scripture enjoins us to dwell in during the Feast of Tabernacles. . . . There is such a thin line between hominess and homelessness, order and chaos, having and losing, life and death. Therefore we need to value all the more what we are loaned, what is ours to enjoy—for how long we do not know."[3]

Many congregants and members of the larger community were actually shocked that ours was the only home singled out for destruction that stormy night. Our response to "Why us?" was "Why not us?" In the days following the fire, I alternated between the belief that God had some purpose beyond my power to fathom and the conclusion that this fire was not God's will but the price of living in a world in which nature follows its natural course. I did feel God's presence that night and during the days to come in our survival, in the strength we received to carry on, in the love of those who embraced and nurtured us, and in my faith that God would empower us to derive a blessing even from this ordeal. In retrospect, this reminder of our vulnerability and neediness was unnerving but, strange as it may seem, also spiritually deepening.

Myrna, a young woman in Houston, read my piece in *The Chronicle* and wrote to tell me about her experience of loss when she was nine years old:

> In January, February, and March of 1952, I lost both my grandfathers and my father very suddenly. Each time, I was at a movie with a friend. A man who worked for the family came to the movie house to tell me that I had to return home. By the third time around, I was wise. I knew what had happened, I just didn't know the who! My mother opened the door and, falling to her knees, told me my father had died. I was nine years old.
>
> You can imagine the turmoil and emotion of the time. One afternoon I went to the hilly park, as it was fondly called,

where I could be alone and cry. I quickly realized that life was
fleeting: that what was here today could be gone tomorrow.
God needed to be eternal and I needed God much more than
God needed me. No choices here, no room for discussion.

Myrna recalled how in the park that day, her utter desolation brought her closer to God. All too often, however, such
moments of spiritual awakening come and pass without
transforming our lives. Somehow, we assume that if we are
receptive to such moments of illumination and we yearn for
spiritual enrichment, we need take no further initiatives of
our own. Inspiration can happen in a flash, but cultivating
habits of mind requires some sort of consistent activity. A
would-be writer can sit and wait for the inspiration to come
so that she can go to the computer and create. But accomplished writers do not usually rely on a spontaneous visit of
the muse. They do extensive research and expose themselves
to experiences that nourish the creative mind. In a disciplined
way, they sit at the computer daily and write. The same holds
for a person who is motivated to lose weight after a heart
attack. Nothing will change unless the moment of inspiration
is followed by a commitment to a routine of diet and exercise that does not rely on random moments of insight.

Earlier I noted that, objectively, the believer and nonbeliever are exposed to the same world. Faith is a particular
way of viewing and receiving the world: to see the birth of a
baby as a gift from God the Creator, or to regard our pursuit
of justice as a response to a God who has shown us the way
we are intended to live, or to experience our liberation from
the "Egypts" of our lives as a sign of God's helping and
redeeming presence.

But what will incline us to see our world through the eyes
of faith? Once again, just opening ourselves to moments of
spiritual awakening is not enough. When a person seeks to

find or reclaim religious faith, I caution them not to rely on the spirit to move them, or to expect a quick fix. No single book, no single act, no inspiring weekend retreat or evening spent listening to a charismatic preacher can bring about instant and enduring spiritual renewal. The way to develop spirituality is through a disciplined journey. Here are some guidelines for that journey that I have drawn from my own experience of Judaism.

Over the years, I have met many persons who have sought spiritual illumination everywhere but in their own spiritual tradition. They assume that spiritual insights have to come from a place that is new, exotic, and far from home. These seekers call to mind a Hasidic tale that I retell here: A poor man named Isaac Yekel lived in a little hut in Cracow. One night he dreamt that in the neighboring city of Prague, across a bridge and within sight of the duke's palace, a great treasure lay buried. When this dream recurred for two successive nights, Isaac Yekel journeyed to Prague with a shovel in hand to search for that treasure.

When he arrived in Prague, he saw the bridge and the road leading to the duke's palace. It was just as it was in his dream. But he also saw soldiers guarding the bridge and the captain of the guard regarded him suspiciously. Taking him for a spy, the guard asked what business brought him to that place. Isaac could only stammer out his true story. Hearing it, the guard burst into laughter, "Did you really come all the way from Cracow believing in a dream? You're crazy! Who believes in dreams? Why, do you know that if I were as silly as you are, I'd be in Cracow myself right now. I dream night after night of a voice telling me there is a treasure waiting for me at the house of a Cracow Jew named Isaac, son of Yekel. Yes, under the stove. Now half the Jews in Cracow probably are named Isaac and the other half named Yekel and they all have stoves! Can you see me going from house to house tearing down the stoves and digging for treasure?"

Isaac thanked the guard, quickly excused himself and hurried back to his home in Cracow. There beneath his own hearth, he discovered the treasure.[4]

This story always reminds me that faith, and the resources of faith, may be nearer to us than we ever supposed, within us or close at hand. Many seekers of faith study New Age spirituality and Eastern religions, but have never encountered the Bible as an adult. There is much to be gained from an inherited religious tradition, but for many of us, our own sacred texts and spiritual practices may seem like the most foreign terrain of all.

If it is prudent to begin the spiritual journey by exploring our given heritage of faith, it is also wise to do so in the company of a supportive community. In our congregation, a confirmation class of teenagers met each Wednesday. Despite our best efforts, class discussion was often limited to a few assertive participants and even they were hesitant to share any thoughts that might expose their vulnerability or not seem "cool" in the eyes of their peers. Many a teenager will not speak of a religious experience in such a setting.

One year we took the confirmation class to a camp in the Texas Hill Country for an annual weekend retreat. By the second day, my colleagues and I were delighted to discover that these young people could openly express religious sentiments. On Sabbath morning, the students wrote their own prayers and were encouraged to share them during the outdoor service. Once the first brave soul spoke up, many others started sharing. Their prayers were self-revealing and soulful. We had created a supportive community in which it was safe to be "uncool" and speak from the heart.

Even as adults, few among us are so self-assured and inner-directed that we fail to be influenced by the company we keep. In a group that disdains "God talk," we are less likely to admit to ourselves, much less to others, that we believe in God, or experience intimations of God's presence, or need to pray. What we allow ourselves to believe or even experience depends significantly on the cultural support for that belief and experience. Peter Berger, a sociologist of religion, speaks of "plausibility structures." Someone who enters and lives in a community of believers is more likely to find belief in God a plausible option.

Changed situations in our lives can also create an opportunity for a new engagement. In the city where they spent most of their lives, David and Gail never joined a synagogue. While they proudly identified with their Jewish heritage, they had no special interest in religious services. For spiritual nourishment, they turned to concerts, museums, dance performances, and theater. Their culture-filled life, they felt, provided all the stimulation they needed.

When they joined a congregation upon moving to a new city, they did so mainly for social reasons; they were new in town and wanted to make friends. They began to come to services on Friday nights. Much to their surprise and delight the cantor's chanting of the Hebrew prayers moved them; they opened their prayer books and willingly joined the congregation in worship. Before long, their weekly attendance was habitual.

On Saturday mornings, they also became regulars at a Torah study discussion group. Both literary people, they eagerly joined the men and women of different ages who gathered to wrestle with the biblical text and the rabbinic commentaries. Soon they readily acknowledged that the Torah study group was more than an intellectual exercise for them; it was a place to find spiritual truth for their own life situations. Attending her first High Holiday services since she was a little girl, Gail found herself sharing her deepest concerns and hopes with a God she wasn't sure she believed in, yet the experience gave her a feeling of peace and comfort.

I do not claim that David and Gail had a dramatic religious conversion experience. But by joining a community for study and worship, they permitted themselves the option of drawing support from religious sources. Here they were able to discover and address spiritual concerns they had never considered before.

A spiritual journey can begin at any stage of life. Herman Gollob's interest in religion grew as he contemplated his retirement from a long and distinguished career in book publishing. How does he explain this late-life hunger for spirituality? In his memoir, *Me and Shakespeare,* Gollob admits that he discovered a hole in his life. His busy, working years, he feels, were characterized by "competitiveness, . . . the self-absorption of careerism, . . . the emotional sterility of operating for the most part in a critical, analytical mode, in the thrall of the intellect."[5] In essence, he had lived the life of the mind but ignored the deepest needs of his heart.

Growing up in a nonreligious Jewish family, Gollob never had a bar mitzvah, though at the insistence of an uncle he went through a perfunctory confirmation service. Seventeen years later, he returned to a synagogue for his wedding ceremony. Although well schooled in Western secular literature, he was totally ignorant of the sacred texts and observances of his religious heritage.

Following his wedding, Gollob managed to avoid the synagogue for another twenty years—until he was invited to the bar mitzvah of a friend's son. Having come only to honor his friend, he was surprised to find that he was more than a passive observer. One of the high points in the Sabbath morning service is the processional in which the Torah scrolls are carried around the congregation before they are unrolled and read. Everyone stands and, as the scrolls are carried passed them, those seated on or near an aisle kiss the fringes of their prayer shawl or prayer book and reach out to touch the Torah. In earlier days, Herman Gollob would have regarded such a ritual as a quaint and interesting custom, but that morning, as he found himself kissing the fringes of his prayer shawl and touching them to the Torah scroll, he knew he had crossed a significant threshold. He began to read books about Judaism and started to observe some of the Sabbath rituals at home. He and his wife joined a neighborhood synagogue, where he began to study for the bar mitzvah he had missed in his youth.

Of his adult bar mitzvah, Gollob writes:

Came the big day, I didn't feel like a performer; holding the Torah, I felt a sense of joy, a mystical sense of being at one with the Divine, and for the first time truly understood that God made his covenant not only with the Israelites but with all the future generations. I was standing at Sinai, with an aching humility and a feeling of innocence and beauty that brought me close to tears frequently during the service.[6]

The study of religious texts provides another supportive forum for spirituality. In Judaism, the study of Torah is considered equal in importance to prayer. With mind and heart, we are invited to immerse ourselves in sacred texts. Many who study such texts, preferably with a teacher and in the company of other students, feel they are in touch with their ancestors and, at times, with the God who inspired them. When Jews gather to study Torah, the tradition teaches, the *Shekhinah*, the indwelling presence of God, is with them.

The Talmud scholar, Rabbi Louis Finkelstein, once observed, "When I pray, I speak to God. When I study Torah, God speaks to me." At the beginning of Torah study, we may declare, "Praised are you, O God, Sovereign of the universe, who teaches Torah to your people."

About an hour before Sabbath morning services, some members of our congregation convene for a Torah study session. They read the weekly Torah portion aloud in English, share what the text says to them, and raise questions for discussion. Often, the participants are able to make vital connections between the biblical text and their own life experiences.

Tamara Green, Professor of Classics at Hunter College, found a healing moment of spiritual illumination in a rabbinic interpretation of a biblical text. For most of her life she has been disabled by a condition that she describes as "not life-threatening but life-encompassing." She cannot walk without crutches and has periodically faced times when her breathing is exceedingly labored. For years she puzzled over the declaration that we are created in the divine image. Bitterly she would ask, "Is then God a cripple?"

In the biblical story of the golden calf, Moses responded to the people's idolatry by smashing the two tablets of the law that he had brought with him (Exodus 32:19). Later we read that Moses returned to the mountain and received a new set of tablets, which were placed in a portable ark (Exodus 34:1). Tamara Green wondered what had happened to the broken tablets. The ancient rabbis asked the same question and responded with this *Aggadah*, "God commanded Moses to place the broken fragments in the ark with those that were whole. The broken ones were to be cherished as much as those that were not broken."[7] At that moment, she had the sense that her Judaism could help her feel cherished and validated. She had just found a healing notion and was now more disposed to experience God's presence in her life.

The path to faith must lead at some point from study to deed. The Torah contains not only sacred stories but also commandments. The Hebrew word *halakhah*, derived from the word "to walk," literally means "the way we are intended to walk through life." The spiritual journey should lead us from the house of study into the world at large.

But what if study does not yield a sense of God's commanding presence? Should we still try to do the deeds commanded? A rabbinic sage imagines God saying, "If they were to forsake me, I should forgive them, for they may yet keep my Torah. For if they should forsake me but keep my Torah, the leaven that is in [the Torah] will bring them closer to me."[8] Doing the commandment can help us feel the presence of God.

In human relationships the sudden strivings of love may inspire acts of devotion. But at times, acts of devotion can profoundly nurture and deepen love. What holds for the human sphere is also true of our relation to the Source of being. When the Israelites stood at Sinai and accepted the covenant, they responded, "All that the LORD has spoken we will faithfully do!" (Exodus 24:7). Many commentators have concluded that only after we *do* a deed do we perceive its spiritual significance.

The Torah commands many deeds that are called *gemilut hasadim*—"acts of lovingkindness." It is a sacred obligation to comfort the sick and those who are in mourning. When we do so, we lessen that preoccupation with ourselves, which is an integral part of our own spiritual growth. Those members of my congregation who regularly visit hospitals and nursing homes, and those who served on the AIDS Care Team felt they were enriched by these low-profile acts of loving-kindness.

The texts of Torah also command *tzedek* or social justice. We are summoned to create a community that protects the most vulnerable among us from exploitation. Joan, a respected community volunteer and activist, puts enormous energy into advocating for society's helpless. She herself is no stranger to life's darker side. She lost a young son in an accident and has battled clinical depression. Some years ago Joan led a grueling but successful legislative effort to protect patients from caregivers who trespass sexual boundaries. She would acknowledge that working for what she believed in drew her closer to the God who commands us, "Do justly." Fulfilling the commandment nourished her spiritually.

Some who feel driven to ease the pain in the world, will say, if pressed, "It makes me feel good. I'm doing it for me, not for them." Such persons may be more religious than they realize. If they probed more deeply why these acts make them feel good, and what sustains them even when their efforts are not appreciated, they may find that doing such deeds helps them discover the meaning and purpose of their life.

Among life's greatest moments of spiritual openness are the times we confront the death of a loved one. For such occasions all religions prescribe rituals of mourning. Jewish mourning rituals encourage us to step aside from the normal rhythm of life, to nurse our loss, and to acknowledge the finality of death. Such mourning rituals include holding prayer services in the home with a *minyan* of ten adults and reciting the Kaddish, the Mourner's Prayer, in the synagogue regularly for eleven months. As a mourner and frequent observer of those in mourning I have experienced the power of reciting the Kaddish. During the week following a funeral, friends gather at an appointed time in the home of the bereaved so they can recite the Kaddish in the presence of at least ten adults. The cadence of the Aramaic words recited aloud (the vernacular of the Near East in the first centuries) and the supportive voices that envelop the mourners are a powerful reminder that they are not alone. The discipline of such ritual obligation offers a semblance of order to a life disrupted by death. Knowing that these words were spoken in similar circumstances by many generations reminds the mourners that they are part of an age-old fellowship of human loss and sorrow.

Perhaps the deepest meaning of the Kaddish ritual is embodied in its ancient Aramaic text that calls upon the mourner to praise and trust God when such trust is most difficult and most needed. Death is the starkest marker of our limited power. When death seems untimely and unfair we must struggle to reaffirm trust in the value of life. At first, we pray the words in order that we may come to believe them. But our hope is that as the months of mourning draw to a close, the words will confirm that we have come to terms with death as part of life.

Literary critic Leon Wieseltier kept a journal during the year he recited the Kaddish for his father, which he published in a book simply called *Kaddish*. Raised in an Orthodox home, Wieseltier had become estranged from the synagogue and from formal prayer. Yet when his father died, he found little solace in a purely intellectual or psychotherapeutic approach to grieving. He knew his father would want him to recite the Kaddish for the traditional eleven-month period of mourning, and found this practice helped him come to terms with his grief over the end of a close but conflicted relationship. Wieseltier writes, "A friend asked why I am saying Kaddish. . . . Because it is my duty to my father. Because it is my duty to my religion. . . . Because the fulfillment of my duty leaves my thoughts about my father unimpeded by regret and undistorted by guilt."[9]

Though a member of my congregation, a man had also grown distant from a religious lifestyle. He began coming to the synagogue every Sabbath morning to recite the Kaddish for his father. Later, he confided to me that what had begun as a filial obligation turned into a significant religious experience for him. When the year of mourning ended, he continued coming to Sabbath worship and Torah study sessions with some regularity.

Ritual discipline is an important, often neglected resource for spiritual growth. On the basis of his cross-cultural studies of religion, anthropologist Clifford Geertz concluded that "ritual observance has been a significant way of engendering religious faith."[10]

The power of ritual has much to do with our disciplined entry into an alternate world with its own rules, language, time frame, and activities. Let me illustrate by first examining one of my very favorite alternate worlds—the world of baseball. (My congregants will attest that some of my best sermon illustrations have been drawn from baseball.) This world has its own language for devotees: fastball, slider, sacrifice fly, double play, seventh inning stretch. Those who attend the game, even more than those who watch at home, enter that world with its rules and definitions of what constitutes victory or defeat. Although baseball is only a game and in some respects far removed from our everyday world, our experience within this alternate world of play enriches and illumines that other world where we live, work, strive, and love.

The same is much more profoundly true of religious ritual. Its rules, special language, and prescribed activities make us conscious of an alternate world that includes but is not exhausted by our world of daily striving. The power of ritual to help us experience that alternate world is most evident in the weekly observance of the Sabbath.

Shabbat (the Hebrew term for the Jewish Sabbath) offers a precious "oasis in time." It is an opportunity to step aside for one day every week from the *striving-doing-making-accomplishing* orientation to the world and see the world as a "created being" rather than a creative one. It is a time to *be* rather than to *do*, a time to renew the body and soul with rest, prayer, religious fellowship, Torah study, and a festive meal. On the Sabbath day, we abstain from work in order to recover our appreciation of the world created by God. Abraham J. Heschel writes that "with our bodies we belong to space. . . . The Sabbath . . . gives us the opportunity to sanctify time."[11]

The Sabbath is therefore a time to place our weekday strivings in perspective. Novelist and playwright Herman Wouk recounts the time when his play *The Caine Mutiny Court Martial* was being rehearsed for its Broadway opening. There were the usual crises and everyone's nerves were frayed. It was Friday afternoon and the play was hardly in shape for the following week's opening. Herman Wouk looked at his watch and realized he had to leave in order to be home in time for the Sabbath. Much to the bewilderment and even consternation of his associates, Wouk left that maelstrom on Broadway for the gentle shelter of home and *Shabbat*. When he returned to the theater on Saturday evening, he was renewed in body and mind and was able to bring a fresh perspective to the problems at hand. The peace and healing of the Sabbath day had enabled him to be a more constructive participant for the remaining days of rehearsal.[12]

In a world of daily hassles, competing obligations, "power lunches," and drivenness to excel, it can be very healing to step off the fast treadmill in order to become centered. We hear much about the need to release stress and become more mindful of our inner world. The Sabbath requires us to stop doing for one day to become more mindful of God's many gifts with joy and gratitude.

I have already suggested the value of sacred story, *Aggadah*, as a means of discovering intimations of God's presence. The Bible records numerous tales of men and women recovering faith and learning to live in the presence of God. In Genesis 28, Jacob flees from home to avoid the violent wrath of his brother, Esau. He finds himself all alone in the wilderness at night. Frightened and weary, he lies down with a stone as his pillow. That night, Jacob dreams of a ladder extending between heaven and earth with angels ascending and descending upon it. God appears and assures him that he is not alone, "I will be with you." When he awakens to the light of day, with courage renewed and hope for the future, Jacob says, "Behold, God is even in this place and I knew it not."

The religious experience of feeling comforted in the presence of God is also reflected in Psalm 23, "Though I walk through the valley of the shadow of death, I will fear no evil, for you are with me." Other psalms reveal the hearts of those who are close to despair, who feel scorned, abandoned, or betrayed by those they trusted. These psalms were written by poets who affirmed the healing presence of *Adonai,* the Lord. The psalmists constantly seek the bedrock of what Christian theologian Paul Tillich called "the courage to be."

The human experience of faith relies on a God who knows our hearts and is with us in our trials. The author of Psalm 41 declares ultimate reliance on God when all others could not be trusted:

> My enemies speak evilly of me,
>   "When will he die and his name perish?"
> If one comes to visit he speaks falsely;
>   his mind stores up evil thoughts;
>   once outside, he speaks them.
> All my enemies whisper together against me,
>   imagining the worst for me.
> "Something baneful has settled in him;
>   he'll not rise from his bed again."
> My ally in whom I trusted,

> even he who shares my bread,
> has been utterly false to me. (Psalm 41:6-10)

But the psalmist concludes that he does not feel alone because of God:

> You will support me because of my integrity,
> and let me abide in Your presence forever.
> Blessed is the LORD, God of Israel,
> from eternity to eternity.
> Amen and Amen. (Psalm 41:13-14)

Like the authors of psalms, we too have had wilderness moments, though perhaps not as dramatically as Natan Sharansky, the Russian Jewish activist who spent years as a "prisoner of conscience" in the Soviet gulag. During long periods of solitary confinement, Sharansky found strength in repeating to himself the words of the Hebrew psalms, especially the phrase, "I will fear no evil / For thou are with me" (Psalm 23). These words enabled him to endure the indignities and injustices he suffered at the hands of his tormentors.[13]

A physician I know experienced an unexpected role reversal—from doctor to patient—when a medical examination revealed that he had cancer. He had to undergo a series of radiation treatments. In a letter to me, he confided that, to his surprise, he was able to overcome a deep sense of isolation and anxiety by repeating the words of the *Sh'ma,* a Jew's primary declaration of faith, "Hear, O Israel, *Adonai* is our God, *Adonai* is One."

For Sharansky and my doctor friend, the prayerful words each spoke in a moment of deepest need lifted to consciousness the awareness that he was not really alone. Why should the pretensions of modernity deprive us of a source of strength we need to live? Like Jacob, we too may discover in moments of utter desolation that "God is even in this place and I knew it not."

Jacob has a different sort of religious experience in chapter 33 of Genesis, when he returns to the land of Canaan twenty years after fleeing from his brother Esau's wrath. He is older now; he has married and raised children. He has cried with them and sometimes because of them. Now a prosperous man, he has done his share of suffering. He had thought his life was settling into a more halcyon rhythm when he was stunned to learn his brother Esau was approaching his encampment with four hundred armed men. Jacob was close to panic. Expecting the worst, he sent his family along with his entourage and his flocks across the river. Meanwhile, he dispatched messengers bearing gifts to meet his brother. Terrified to come face-to-face with his aggrieved brother, Jacob prayed for divine deliverance.

Then we read of a great showdown worthy of the heightened tension in the classic western *High Noon*. Jacob bows seven times as he sees Esau coming toward him to signal his submission to his brother. In the animal kingdom, signals of submission disarm the more powerful adversary and avoid violence. In the human species, however, such gestures do not function instinctively. Jacob was afraid.

And what did Esau do? He ran to greet his brother. Esau embraced and kissed Jacob and they wept. Jacob must have been both stunned and grateful. He expected the worst and was surprised by a moment of unbelievable grace. Shortly thereafter, Jacob implored Esau to accept his gifts because "to see your face is like seeing the face of God" (Genesis 33:10).

This episode is not the wilderness experience of being alone yet not alone. Here, God appears in the face of another person. A person who appears in our lives when we most need help and heals, rather than hurts, becomes a mirror of the face of God. We have all been on the receiving and giving ends of such encounters.

A friend of mine illustrates this "face of God" experience in poetry. He alludes to a traumatic series of events in his life that threatened to overwhelm him, using the imagery of struggling in a raging sea:

A powerful wave
Overwhelmed me,
The undertow
Pulled me out to sea.
Trauma—
Wave and undertow.
Not alone
The blow
The loss
The challenge,
But the ebbing of self
The pain of soul
The pulling apart of me.
Wave and undertow.
My self swept out to sea—
Another name for death.
Yet here I am.
You have gathered me through,
Whole and strong again.

Your precious dolphins,
My wife and children,
And an old friend,
With love and wisdom
Bearing me toward shore.

How did my friend experience God's delivering presence? His family and other people were the face of God for him at a critical point in his life. Each of us can become God's messengers when we appear at just the right time to heal, comfort, and love.

I'll never forget a call from the friend of a congregant named Joe who was scheduled to enter the hospital on a certain day for surgery. The friend suggested I call him because he knew that Joe wanted to talk with me but doubted whether he would take the initiative. I called, but no one was home.

That day, I had to conduct a funeral in our congregational cemetery. After completing the graveside service, I decided to go home via a different and purportedly shorter route. I made a wrong turn and could see the highway but not how to enter it, which for me is not unusual. After driving lost for a while, I ended up on my usual route and decided to stop at a favorite cafeteria for lunch. As I sat down with my tray and looked up, the man I had called and missed earlier that morning was standing beside me.

"Joe, aren't you going to the hospital?" I asked.

"Yes, but I decided to eat my favorite pasta before admitting myself."

He sat down and we talked. If I hadn't been lost for half an hour and deviated from my daily routine, this accidental meeting would not have happened. I have never had a stronger sense of being where I was intended to be and doing what I was intended to do. As for Joe, though he did not use those words, it was clear from his face that meeting me at that moment was "like seeing the face of God."

Leave aside the statistical probability of our converging as we did in the fourth largest city in the country; leave aside whether this meeting was more than "coincidence"—someone has said coincidence is God's way of remaining anonymous— this much is beyond question: our meeting was a special experience for each of us. Sometimes we can feel God's presence through other human beings and coincidences such as this. If we permit ourselves to label and receive such experiences as religious, they can also renew our faith.

There are many ways to recover a religious orientation to life and its gift of healing. We need not do all the identical deeds or respond to all the same stories. There is room for experimentation and individuation. There are paths that await us in study, ethical deeds, religious fellowship, and ritual. If we wish to discover the healing power of a religious tradition and recover the gift of faith, we will expend significant time and energy along the way. Few if any who devote themselves to the quest will be disappointed. Perhaps that is what is meant by the words of the psalmist, "The LORD is near to all who call Him" (Psalm 145:18).

Chapter 5

Prayer—The Vital Connection

When I went out towards you, I found you coming towards me.
—Judah Halevi

YEARS AGO, WHEN I was just starting out as a rabbi, I encountered a psychiatrist who was afflicted with cancer. When I first entered his hospital room he was sullen, uncommunicative, and angry. He greeted my questions and efforts at conversation with a stony silence and an unfriendly stare. The more I returned, however, the more he seemed to welcome my presence. Over the weeks of our visits he became more talkative and openly appreciative of my visits. We became friends.

Once, before I left the room, my friend assured me he was about to confide a secret he had not shared with anyone, not even his wife or his children. He extracted a promise that I would not reveal his secret even at the funeral service he expected me to conduct. He then confessed he was a closet pray-er. Not a day passed since his youth when he did not engage in some prayer. Why was this such a deep secret? Prayer, he thought, conflicted with the scientific rationalism demanded by his professional role. (In today's cultural climate, a psychiatrist would feel less pressure to keep his faith in the closet.) My congregant's embarrassed confession reminded me there are those who pray, but secretly. No doubt many more of us pray than publicly admit it.

At certain points in each of our lives, we realize the extent to which we are limited human beings. In moments of trouble and pain we become most fully aware that we are not masters of our destiny. We may have tried our best to raise good kids, yet feel defeated by the paths they have taken. We work hard to build a business only to discover market forces have conspired to defeat us. We think we are taking good care of our bodies only to be shocked by the onset of serious illness. We may be successful superachievers yet one setback can catapult us into a frenzy of self-hate. When that happens, it is hard to say which is worse, the defeat, or how it makes us feel about ourselves.

In a provocative little book titled *God and the New Haven Railway*, George O'Brien reminds us of our favorite human response to frustration: we curse. Our muttering of those unprintable four-letter words is an expression of life's frustrations, including being stuck on a delayed New Haven commuter train on Friday afternoon. O'Brien writes, "Cursing and prayer . . . are both forms of discourse which are addressed to powers out of human control. . . . In pure cursing, the power is invoked with some destructive intent; pure prayer invokes for more creative or sustaining ends."[1]

We are more given to prayer at moments when we come face-to-face with situations that are beyond our control. A nonreligious congregant will confess, "Rabbi, I've even prayed a lot the last few days." Trouble, often accompanied by a sense of helplessness, is the classic parent of prayer. We pray before we take our feeble human initiatives and we pray after we've done all that we can and realize anew that we need help from a power beyond us.

On a plane bound for New York I was preparing a sermon on the psalms. As we glided over the clouds in our man-made flying machine I read Psalm 121. The unknown author of that particular psalm probably referred to the Judean hills, looking, upward and exclaiming, "I lift up my eyes to the mountains. From where does my help come?" Acknowledging his littleness, the psalmist declared, "My help comes from the LORD, / maker of heaven and earth" (Psalm 121:2).

I didn't have to look up at the mountains; I was flying over them. How can those hills still mediate my sense of limitedness when I soar over them at an altitude of 31,000 feet and a ground speed of 500 miles per hour? Ask the same question of an astronaut and he or she will tell you that even when you have managed to fly hundreds of thousands of miles above the earth, you are still assaulted by a sense of littleness in the immensities of space. The child who lies on the ground on a clear night and is bedazzled by the canopy of the stars shares with the astronaut, the commercial airline passenger, and the biblical poet an encounter with our lack of control or self-sufficiency.

After we landed, I was given a more mundane metaphor for my lack of full control. As we left the airport, the cab got into heavy traffic. I was late for my meeting. The cab driver cursed persistently, honked his horn in anger, and maneuvered his vehicle through any miniscule space he could seize.

The ancient shepherd looked up at the hills, blew his *shofar* and experienced his creatureliness. The New York cab driver blew his electronic horn into the sea of cars around him and knew he too was not fully master of his destiny. Not only mountains but other persons whose goals and interests conflict with our own (as in the sea of New York traffic) also remind us that we human creatures are dependent on forces beyond our control.

What is the most compelling symbol of our creatureliness? In the psalmist's ancient Judea, as in America at the beginning of the twenty-first century, nothing signals human limits with greater clarity than the transience of life itself. I sit here cozily ensconced in our little cottage in northern Michigan where for over thirty years we have spent a portion of each summer. My wife and I have come to mark the passage of the years by these summers in Charlevoix. As we get older, summer arrives and departs ever more rapidly. Each year we ask, "Where did it all go?" Long before us, the psalmist lamented that we are like the grass: "In the morning it flourishes and grows, in the evening it is cut down and withers." The author of Psalm 90 acknowledges, "They pass by speedily, and we are in darkness."

All attempts to deny the contingency of our human existence are futile or self-deceptive. Neither drugs nor rampant promiscuity nor the most elaborate schemes of self-aggrandizement nor cosmetic strategies for eternal youthfulness will shield us from the naked truth. Even the most secular nonbeliever is aware that our lives are "as a passing shadow."

In our creatureliness we grope for an ultimate reliance. No human being can provide that unshakable ground of trust for us because each person is himself or herself caught up in the world of essential finitude. How shattering is the moment of truth when the parent we thought would always be there for us is dying. After she had experienced the death of two grandparents and a father within three months, Myrna at age nine had concluded, "God needed to be eternal, and I needed God much more than God needed me."

Of course, there are other possible conclusions we can draw. Many thinkers over the course of centuries have concluded that we are indeed dependent upon a power greater than our own but that power (or those powers) cannot be trusted to care about us or help us cope with life. According to this view we live at best in a world indifferent to our human needs and hopes; at worst, we are confronted by a power that is, like the killer whale in *Moby Dick,* "an inscrutable malice." We must simply huddle with fellow sojourners on this earth and tough it out with no invisible means of support.

Whether we counter our essential limitedness by reaching out to God or surmise that there is no caring presence in the world is more a matter of faith than empirical experience. Even when we pray, moments of wondering if there is anyone there may alternate with moments when we feel that God is "closer to us than breathing."

God's presence may come in various forms. In her account of birthing and living with a child with Down syndrome, Martha Beck, author of *Expecting Adam,* writes of a time when she did more praying than she had done in her entire previous adult life. She recalls an extremely anxious time just prior to going into labor. Her mind had been overwhelmed with fearful thoughts of all that could go wrong in this abnormal pregnancy. Her fear dissolved when the room became suffused with light, which she experienced as almost a physical presence:

> When the being disappeared, leaving a residue of love on every surface of my apartment, my uterus was still contracting enthusiastically. But my fear, and the sense of pitched battle, were gone. I no longer worried about going into labor. I felt utterly trustful that things were under control, though no control of mine.[2]

The Jewish tradition does not expect us to defer our praying individually or in community until we have neatly resolved all our theological questions about the presence or absence of God. Prayer is one of those divine commandments we do in order to discover the validity of what we have done. We pray that we may be able to pray. Before reciting the *Amidah*—the central prayer of a Jewish worship service—the worshiper recites, "O God, open my lips that my mouth may declare your glory." The ability to pray is also a gift for which we are grateful.

Many millions of people in our time as in ages past have felt the need for prayer. Guided by spiritual mentors or driven by their own desperation, they prayed because they needed to pray. Those virtuosos of prayer who wrote the psalms countered their sense of human limits with faith, at times confirmed by experience, that the decisive Power in the universe is a caring God who hears us and may respond. Prayer is our vital connection to the Source of being.

In the opening chapters of the book of Samuel, Hannah is overwhelmed with anguish over her barrenness. She prays to God for a child. We assume she and her husband, Elkanah, enacted their human roles in the drama of conception, but Hannah's barrenness remained. In her desperation she went to the sanctuary and prayed. As it happened her prayers were answered. A child was born to Hannah and her husband within a year of her special plea. They called him Samuel, which means, "I asked the Lord for him."

Today, a couple with problems of fertility would consult a physician who has specialized in such problems and would no doubt receive some medications and guidance for the next attempts to conceive. During that anxious period of doing and waiting one or both of them may pray regularly. If at some point they are informed that conception has occurred, and they were asked to define God's role in this event, they might conclude that God answered their prayers through the skill of their physician and the efficacy of those fertility pills.

Of course, the Bible (and later the rabbis) make a much bolder claim. In those days there were no fertility clinics or biochemically synthesized drugs. Desperate for a child, Hannah simply went to the sanctuary and tearfully offered her prayers. She vowed that if blessed with a son she would dedicate him to God's service. In this story, God, not any mediating priest or herb, is the sole healer of her barrenness.

Such a claim might violate our sense of scientific rationalism. Yet most of us have experienced personally, or through someone we know, instances when a physical healing appears to be unexpected or even unexplainable in medical terms. Even some doctors acknowledge these feelings. In his book *God, Faith, and Health,* Dr. Jeff Levin recounts a time when he was a graduate student at the University of Texas Medical Branch in Galveston. He was rushing down a street during a vicious thunderstorm when he slipped and fell. X-rays revealed that his spine was not damaged, but he had a couple of cracked ribs:

> The doctor on call told me it would probably take about six weeks for my ribs to fully heal. To add to my misery, I had injured the bursae in both elbows, and my arms were locking up in a half-bent position. That, too, I was told, could take quite a while to return to normal.[3]

After being given slings for both arms, he was told that nothing else could be done medically and was discharged. Feeling weak and helpless, he still had to face the added stress of studying for his comprehensive exams, the last hurdle before qualifying for his PhD. Jeff called his parents in Chicago and gave vent to his despair. His mother, who was a participant in an interfaith prayer group, asked her friends to pray for her son's speedy recovery. About two dozen people in different parts of the country were praying for Jeff that evening.

When Jeff awoke the next morning, he was surprised to find that he felt intact.

> Without thinking I rolled out of bed and extended my arm to reach for the light, just like any other day. It took a second to

realize what I had done, and I fell back in shock. My cracked ribs were almost entirely better. I could breathe fully, I had full upper-body movement, and there was only the slightest twinge of pain when I took my fist and pounded it into my side as a test. . . . After midday meditation and a brief nap, I awoke completely healed.[4]

Jeff recalls that "six-week convalescence prayed down to a day and a half" was a sign of God's response to all the prayers that were said for his quick recovery.

Before commenting, let me share an experience still closer to home. It concerns an unusual experience I shared with a couple from our congregation, Jim and Beverly. At my request, Jim later sent me this e-mail recapping what had happened:

We brought Beverly to the hospital that Monday for observation, with irregularities with her heart. Later that night, she was moved to the ICU as heart failure had occurred. At the time of your arrival the next day she had experienced massive heart failure [requiring an implant of a heart pump] . . . her condition was critical, with "touch and go" as ongoing status. She had not been conscious since Monday evening.

When I visited the hospital that Tuesday afternoon, I prayed with the family and then accompanied Jim to Beverly's bedside in the ICU. Jim recalls the scene:

You placed your palm on her forehead and recited in Hebrew a prayer for healing. Beverly responded immediately by opening her eyes. Then she said, "Sam, how nice of you to come to see me." . . . You then asked her if she would like to join you in reciting the *Sh'ma*. As you started she joined word for word. I was so overwhelmed I could not continue with the verse. Upon completion she closed her eyes and fell into a deep sleep. . . . We described the experience to my family and they too felt something exceptional might have occurred. Later that night I felt for the first time Beverly was going to make it. I have relived this experience many times. I can neither rationalize nor understand anything more today than I did when it occurred. However, I do believe there was a demonstration of how prayer (with deep religious faith) can be answered.

Weeks after this event, Jim affirmed the power of that experience:

This has made a significant impact in both of our lives. We see how fragile every life is. We assume much less, take less for granted, loving each other more than ever, making more of every day we have, and recognizing that in some strange way there is a God and God does hear our prayers. We both thank God very often for a second chance at life.

What shall we make of such experiences? I too was surprised. I am a man of faith, not a faith healer. Was Beverly's awakening just a timely coincidence, or a little miracle? In recent years, I have become much more open to phenomena that elude rational or scientific explanations and I find that I am not alone. Commenting on faith in a postmodern age, theologian Eugene Borowitz observes, "We have begun turning to God for what God might independently do for the ill. And sometimes we find that God heals in ways we must call God's own."[5] The recovery of this more traditional view of prayer has revitalized my private devotion. When I ask for physical healing for people I care for, I believe that God hears prayer and that God may answer prayer—not only by sending us physicians and effective medical interventions and endowing our bodies with a natural capacity for healing—but in ways that we simply must call God's own.

Those incidents of prayer and healing are notable because so many times we pray to God for a physical healing and are not answered. We have all experienced unanswered prayers, and surely such times call for faith in a God whose ways are beyond our full understanding. But we who have prayed may discover that even if the objective source of our trouble is not removed, we have been affected by the very act of praying.

In times of trouble we have a gut-wrenching need to tell our story. If we are fortunate, our parents were accessible listeners to the stories we needed to share as children. Some were "horror stories" of things that happened in school. Later in life, we tell our spouses the "horror stories" from work. Even when the listener cannot undo what has occurred or remove the source of trouble, we often feel better for having shared our pain with another who we believe really cares and loves us. The connection to that person is itself a means of healing.

Extending the metaphor, prayer is a time of intimate sharing with our divine parent. The author of Psalm 147 speaks of God as the One who "heals their broken hearts, / and binds up their wounds." There is healing in sharing what has happened to us and how we feel about it with one who listens and cares. If through prayer we sense that we are not alone, and are given intimations of God's presence, we have received a most precious gift.

At its core, healing is the recovery of wholeness and inner peace. Healing is not confined to physical cure; it may simply be the discovery of the courage we did not have before. Dorothy Bernard said, "courage is fear that has said its prayers." Healing may be the recovery of trust that there is a God and, as the biblical Jacob declared at a time of need, "God is even in this place and I did not know it."

Sometimes adversity brings out our faith. Susan was an attractive, energetic middle-aged woman who was active in the Jewish community but did not consider herself a religious Jew until she learned she had a serious illness. The initial diagnosis of a rare cancer shattered her emotionally. As she sought various consultations and rode the roller coaster of discouragement and hope, Susan felt an intense need to draw closer to her religion. We met and talked regularly. She read some materials I had given her and she prayed. She told me she felt God's nearness much more than she ever thought she could or would. She spoke of an inner peace. The night before her surgery, Susan was surrounded by family and a few dear friends, who, at her request celebrated her birthday in her hospital room. It was a poignant occasion. Considering the uncertainties she faced, she seemed amazingly at peace. The next morning, the family, gathered in the waiting room, learned that Susan had died on the operating table. Sadly, she was not cured, but I believe she did experience a healing of spirit in those last weeks of her life.

Judaism distinguishes situations in which prayer can bring a full healing from those circumstances when "the decree has been sealed." If a point has been reached when it is not God's will (or in God's power) to reverse a terminal condition or chronic illness, should we continue to pray or is prayer at that point futile? This question is raised in the Talmud. According to one talmudic sage named Rabbi Isaac, "Crying out to God in supplication is good for a person whether before the decree has been sealed or after."[6]

What Rabbi Isaac is saying, it seems to me, is that sometimes when we pray we will be healed in body and spirit and sometimes we will be healed in spirit even when we can't be healed in body. Prayer may enable us to live meaningfully in the face of conditions we cannot change. We are also healed in spirit if we are able to be grateful for blessings we have received in this life even when we know our life on earth is drawing to a close.

Rabbi Pinhas of Koretz relates his visit with Rabbi Israel, the Master of the Good Name, as the master was lying on his deathbed. Most disciples had obeyed Rabbi Israel's wish and returned home, but Rabbi Pinhas remained with him. When Pinhas began to pray for a physical healing, Rabbi Israel whispered, "Too late, Pinhas. What is done is done, what is done will not be undone."[7] I would like to believe that Pinhas continued to pray for his master, though he may have changed the words of his prayer.

Some psalm prayers are pleas for reconciliation with a God from whom the author feels estranged. Psalm 51 asks for God's help in getting back on the right track, "Fashion a pure heart for me, O God; / create in me a steadfast spirit. / Do not cast me out of Your presence, / or take Your holy spirit away from me" (51:12-13).

We moderns are uneasy with the notion of suffering as the wages of sin. We prefer to think of God as nurturer rather than judge and we know that the world is full of undeserved suffering. When, in a difficult time, we ask, "What did I do to deserve this?" much of the time the appropriate answer is nothing. Yet we would not want to live in a world where there is no accountability and judgment. Moreover, there are times when we cannot deny that some of our problems are of our own making. We may have harmed our health through less than ideal habits; we may have ruptured relationships through insensitive words or deeds. Such patterns of living are often not without consequences, but we are no less needful of support when we are trying to make changes in the way we live our lives.

All the great religious traditions have prayer rituals that are intended to help us change and elevate the quality of our lives. In Judaism, the High Holiday season, from Rosh Hashanah to Yom Kippur, is the preeminent time to take an inventory of the soul and see ourselves as God sees us. In our prayers, we acknowledge that we need help from a power greater than ourselves to change the course of our lives. But the rabbinic tradition also teaches that before we can ask forgiveness from God, we must first ask forgiveness from those we have alienated.

With each passing year, Judy felt a greater sadness at the High Holiday season because she and her older sister were estranged. Their hardened grievances resulted in coldly correct behavior at family gatherings and total avoidance the rest of the time. A combination of self-righteousness, pride, and fear of rejection prevented Judy from taking the initiative toward reconciliation.

One Rosh Hashanah, the liturgy affected her very deeply. In the moments of silent meditation, she found herself asking for God's help in ending this estrangement. That afternoon, when the family gathered at an uncle's home, Judy felt the usual sense of walking on eggs in her sister's presence. After a round of small talk, she asked her sister if they could speak privately in an adjoining room. After a short, awkward silence, she felt empowered to express her sadness at their distance. She acknowledged her share in causing the rift between them and asked for her sister's forgiveness. Her sister responded as did Esau to Jacob. Without another word, she embraced her sister. They kissed and wept. From that day, they have worked toward restoring a closeness both sisters wanted but had denied themselves. Judy's prayer had given her the courage to take the first steps.

There is another aspect of prayer called *teshuvah*, which means turning to God as an active power in our lives. The Hasidic rabbi, Mendel of Kotzk, was once asked, "Where is God?" He replied, "Wherever man lets God in."[8] God is ever active to create, heal, and redeem, but God has so fashioned us that God can do more for us when we open ourselves to the nourishing energy of our creator. Prayer is our way of turning toward God.

Even if we accept our ultimate dependence on God, God can only act when allowed into our lives. God may always be doing everything possible to heal, liberate, and empower us, but human beings are creatures endowed with freedom and dignity. Therefore, God's helping presence in our lives depends on our openness and responsiveness. The sun nourishes the plant because the plant turns naturally and inexorably toward its rays. We are not simply a part of the world of nature. We can choose to turn toward or away from God. We need God's nourishment no less than the plant but we may turn away from the Source of our being.

Dr. Bernie Siegal, the Yale surgeon and author of *Love, Medicine, and Miracles,* has taught that, because of the interdependence of body, mind, and spirit, the patient's inner peace, trust, and hope may critically affect the outcome of biomedical intervention. A hopeful patient may do better in surgery and respond better to chemotherapy than one who has given up hope. Apart from the fact that we pray at such times because we need to pray, it is also true that by our prayers we become partners in the healing process, along with the physician and God, the ultimate healer.

Dew—that delicate moisture we find on the earth's surface at dawn—is a symbol of healing. The prophet Isaiah said, "For Your dew is like the dew on fresh growth; / You make the land of the shades come to life" (26:19). Moved by this imagery, Rabbi Nina Beth Cardin has written a prayer for the taking of chemotherapy. I have said this prayer as I sat with patients who were frightened by this scary and unpleasant procedure:

> Merciful one, open the gates of your wondrous storehouse,
> releasing your sparkling dew. . . .
> Droplets of dew, come for a blessing not a curse.[9]

Through prayers such as this, we affirm that the power within us, the healing acts of the physician, and the efficacy of the medicine we receive are all gifts of the Source of all Being. We also open ourselves to God's direct healing. We lift our consciousness to meet God's healing presence.

One of the most poignant parts in a Jewish worship service is the recitation of a prayer called the *Misheberech*, when we pray for God's healing upon those who are ill, "May the One who blessed Abraham, Isaac, and Jacob [and some add the matriarchs, Sarah, Rebecca, Leah, and Rachel], bless . . . and deliver this person from trouble and distress, from affliction and illness." On request the name of the person who is ill is said aloud publicly. Many of us will tell the person, "We said a *Misheberech* for you" or "You have been in our prayers."

At the very least, through such intercessory prayers we convey to the person that his or her well-being is important to us, important enough to pray for. Anyone who hears that they have been in our prayers will be deeply moved. But people who have engaged in what we call "intercessory prayer" have felt that their prayers were heard and that they contributed to the healing of sick friends even if they were not aware that prayers were offered on their behalf. I don't doubt this claim.

In an attempt to correlate the claims of faith and science, Dr. Larry Dossey and others have made an effort to prove the efficacy of intercessory prayer by scientific means.[10] Although I am a religious believer who prays frequently, I cannot share their enthusiasm for these efforts. God's ways are more subtle, unknowable, and unpredictable than such demonstrations would suggest. Faith by its very nature is not susceptible to scientific proof or it wouldn't be faith. The God I believe in does not submit to our experimental designs.

Faith is trivialized when it depends upon a predictable flow of tangible rewards. Sometimes we believe because of what we experience and sometimes we believe in spite of what we experience. Sometimes we believe our prayers have been answered and sometimes we believe despite the fact that they were not answered, or at least not answered according to our desire.

Essentially, we pray for ourselves and others not because we have unmistakable guarantees of predictable results—we pray because we need to pray. We pray because we have some intimation that we are connected to a power greater than ourselves. And we pray because we believe, or want to believe, in a God who knows us and cares for us.

Each morning, before I begin my workday, I take twenty minutes for personal prayer. I allow myself to be nourished by the traditional Jewish prayer book, choosing those prayers prescribed for recitation at the beginning of the day. Through these prayers I sense my connection to generations of my people who, in community or alone, voiced their gratitude for God's gifts, their dependence on God's power and love, and their hopes for the future. At certain points, the worshiper is encouraged to set aside the given text and offer prayers that flow from the heart.

In my own devotions I use the traditional Jewish texts selectively, choosing those prayers that express what I feel. I allow time to share with God my gratitude and yearnings. Yet, as important as this experience is to me, let me confess that I have never gotten through the standard prayers without some mental distraction. I have never remained totally focused on the words and their meanings. Intermittently unrelated thoughts invade my consciousness. The rabbinic sages recognized this challenge when they spoke of moments of full concentration *(kavanah)*, as opposed to the moments when we read certain prayers as if we are on automatic pilot. Wisely, the rabbis did not suggest that we pray only if we can be totally focused. If we were to pray only when the spirit moved us, we would probably abandon the discipline of prayer. There is value in setting aside time to recite those prayers even if moments of full presence alternate with moments of distraction.

Meditation is often associated with the mystics' yearning to intensify the spiritual experience in prayer and, as much as possible, to bridge the separation between us and our Creator. To this end, meditation seeks first to overcome the flood of uninvited thoughts that distract us. Its goal is to help us let go of the random smorgasbord of distracting thoughts that pop in and out of our minds. Many mystics call this state of internal disorder "monkey mind" because as Rabbi David Cooper explains, "Our thoughts seem to jump rapidly as though from one branch to another."[11] The practice of meditation aims to overcome "monkey-mind" and heighten our awareness in the present moment.

Cooper, a contemporary mystic and leader of meditation retreats, explains how meditators were taught to focus their minds. Sometimes attention is focused on a visualized object or a single word or phrase. When random thoughts do threaten to disrupt our concentration, the meditator is instructed to calmly dismiss them. As he or she is able to quiet the mind, awareness fills the vacuum. While the initial goal is to heighten our consciousness of self, a higher goal for the religious meditator is to lose the boundary between self and non-self. Cooper describes his experience of meditation, "There is no separation between 'me' and 'not me' between subject and object. . . . The feeling within is a constant 'at oneness,' nothing separate, nothing to ponder, everything in its place, as it should be, just right, perfect. To say that this is the most complete peace is an understatement."[12]

For the religious mystic, the ultimate goal is not only unification with the world but with God. Rabbi Joseph Karo, a sixteenth-century Jewish mystic, gives this advice for the prayer-meditation experience:

Nullify every thought that enters your heart. . . . Unify your heart constantly, at all times, so that every instant you will think of nothing other than God, [God's] Torah and [God's] worship. This is the mystery of Unity, through which a person literally unifies himself with his Creator. The soul attaches itself to [God], and becomes one with [God], so that the body literally becomes a dwelling place of the Divine Presence. [13]

Let me confess that I am neither a mystic nor a meditator. I do seek to combat distracting thoughts as I recite the traditional prayers and express the thoughts and feelings of my heart. While I seek to open myself to God's presence and to feel God's nearness, I do not seek to lose my sense of self in relation to the world or God. In prayer I may experience an intimation of God's presence and nearness but I remain me and God remains God. My goal is dialogue, not unity.

Fortunately, there are different paths to deeper faith. For many contemporary seekers, the path of meditation and mysticism have been spiritually enriching. Some contemporary prayer services have incorporated a period for meditation to heighten self-awareness and allow for a greater degree of personal prayer within the hour of worship.

At the beginning of David Cooper's book *A Heart of Stillness,* he describes a more modest goal for meditation, which I would endorse as a goal of my own prayer discipline:

Part of the spiritual path is to be reminded of things we already know. We forget our lessons so easily. Life is too busy. It tends to overwhelm us. If we get caught in the swirl, we lose our balance. So we must give ourselves an opportunity to quiet down on regular occasions, to reflect, and to remember who we are, what we are doing here, what we have promised ourselves, and where we are going.[14]

Even if prayer simply gives us an opportunity to reflect on and adjust our priorities—to consider what is truly important to us and give thanks—that alone would suffice.

The primary impulse to prayer is the awareness that we are not fully in control. Our neediness and vulnerability are the deepest roots of prayer. But what of those other times in life when we do not feel needy or vulnerable? Our health is excellent; things are going quite well, thank you. We bask in the love of our life partner, take pride in the achievements of our children, and experience success and satisfaction in our work. We seem to be at the peak of our powers. We are on a roll. Whether this great time in our life is deemed the fruit of our abilities, or an entitlement, or dumb luck, we are in a mode of self-sufficiency and feel very much in control. Where then is the impulse to pray?

Such a time does not inspire prayers for divine help and support. But what about prayers of praise and thanksgiving? The truth is that we human creatures are more inclined to ask God for what we need than to thank God for what we have. We are more likely to pray when circulation problems threaten our existence than to thank God for this day of health and strength. New parents are more naturally inclined to pray in the midst of a perilous delivery than to offer thanksgiving after a normal birth. Yet at the very core of a spiritually aware life is a cultivated sense of wonder and gratitude. Such gratitude may lead to prayer that acknowledges we are the receivers of precious gifts from the Source of Being.

Since such prayers come to us less naturally, we need a spiritual discipline of prayer that enhances the awareness of our gifts. The Jewish tradition developed a magnificent discipline of prayer benedictions for every occasion. Each begins with the phrase, "Praised be thou, O God, Ruler of the universe, who . . . " Each such benediction is a prayer of praise, an acknowledgment that we are the receivers of God's good gifts.

Upon awakening, a Jew is instructed to recite these words: "I thank you living and eternal God for having restored my soul in your kindness; how great is your faithfulness." Israel Ibn-Al-Nakawa, a fourteenth-century Spanish rabbi, explained that each night's surrender to slumber is a kind of dying, each awakening a renewal of the gift of life. Hence, we pray, "I thank you living and eternal God for having restored my soul in your kindness."

The Talmud teaches that a faithful Jew should recite at least one hundred such benedictions daily.[15] Before we eat we should say, "Praised be thou, O God, Ruler of the universe who brings forth bread from the earth." If we see a tree in bloom, "Praised is the one who left nothing missing in the world." When we encounter a person of lovely appearance, "Praised be the One who created such as these in this world."

A prayer text for morning devotions praises God for creating the human creature in wisdom and specifically mentions the marvelous network of bodily vessels and orifices that make our natural functions possible. This prayer is designated for recitation after leaving the commode. (Yes, there is an earthiness to Jewish prayer.) Never did that prayer seem more resonant to me than the week following prostate surgery when my catheter was removed and I discovered I could exercise some control over my natural functions. With fullness of heart I recited the prescribed words of praise to God, "We praise the eternal God, sovereign of the universe, who with wisdom has fashioned us. . . . Were even one of these organs to fail, we could not stand alive before You."[16]

Dr. Kenneth Prager wrote in *The Journal of the American Medical Association* about the case of Josh, a twenty-year-old student who sustained a spinal cord injury in a car accident. Early on there were signs of neurological recovery. With good medical care and a superb physical therapist Josh made great progress. But he still required intermittent catheterization and that seemed destined to be his life situation. "One day," Dr. Prager writes, "the impossible happened. I was there the day Josh no longer required a urinary catheter." In response to the moment, he invited Josh to recite that traditional Jewish benediction, and he writes, "As he recited the ancient *bracha* [prayer], tears welled in my eyes. Josh is my son."[17]

I doubt that too many of my ancestors recited one hundred benedictions of formal praise to God each day or that many even had on the tip of their tongues the benediction that was appropriate for any given life experience. But if they prayed the prescribed morning service either in the privacy of their homes or in a congregation of fellow worshipers, they encountered daily opportunities to praise and thank their creator. Far fewer of us engage in the daily discipline of such formal prayer or even private personal meditation, but I heartily recommend a discipline of daily prayer to the spiritual seekers and to all who yearn for spiritual sustenance in their life journey.

As with any structured activity, sometimes the recitation of prayer will be routine and at other times the words will trigger an awareness of blessings too easily taken for granted. Years ago, having newly recovered from an episode of immobilizing back spasms, I found especially resonant a morning prayer which I had recited thousands of times before without an equivalent feeling of appreciation, "Praised are you, O God . . . who enables the bent to stand erect."

I will never forget the tingling within my soul one morning at a youth camp when I sat in an outdoor chapel for morning devotions. I was sandwiched in between two of my young daughters. Each was so close I could feel their pulse. At that very moment the prayer recited aloud by the congregation was, "Praised are you, O God, who renews daily the work of creation." That morning I consciously received the living presence of my daughters as a renewed gift.

It is all too human to be aware of blessings only after they have departed. Does God need our praise and thanksgiving? Whatever our response, this much is certain: We need to thank and praise God to fully cherish the gift of life.

Years ago I visited a middle-aged woman after she underwent brain surgery. Tearfully, she described her husband's first visit to the recovery room when he held her hand and said, "I didn't realize how much I love you until I was afraid I lost you." In the midst of the draining burden of serious surgery and the prospect of an extended convalescence this woman counted her blessings. We recited together *Shecheheyanu,* that great prayer of praise and thanksgiving, "Praised are you, O God, Ruler of the universe, who has kept us in life, sustained us, and permitted us to reach this moment."

Prayers of praise and thanksgiving are rooted in the conviction that *miracle* is not a word reserved only for occasions when the preemie in the incubator defies the statistical odds and survives. The moment when any child is eased out of the womb and utters his or her first cry is also a miracle. Thus our liturgy wisely invites us to thank God for "Your miracles that are with us everyday." The discipline of prayer helps nourish that sense of wonder that Rabbi Abraham Joshua Heschel called "radical amazement." Such wonder is at the heart of a life of the spirit. A life without wonder and gratitude is spiritually barren.

When a prayer discipline includes both petitions for what we lack and thanksgiving for what we have, we are better armed to cope with life's darker side. If we thank God for the good things, we may be better equipped to face the trials that confront us. If even in the hour of trouble we remember to acknowledge our blessings, we may be more able to maintain our belief that life, for all its pain, is worth the price. That affirmation is the key to recovering the gift of meaning and healing.

Chapter 6

Overcoming a Crisis of Faith

For you have striven with beings divine and human,
and have prevailed. —Genesis 32:29

HOW GREAT IT WOULD be if we could always believe that God is an infinite, caring presence, who is unfailingly there for us in time of need. The sober truth is that at times we are unable to experience God even when we reach out in prayer. Pinhas of Koretz taught that when God appears to be hiding God's face, "It ceases to be a hiding if you know it is a hiding." In our crises of the spirit we may fear, not that God is hiding, but that there is no God.

In such moments, I have found some comfort knowing that even the great giants of the Jewish spirit experienced such crises. Pinhas of Koretz certainly did and so did Rabbi Nahman of Bratslav, the nineteenth-century Hasidic rabbi known for his enigmatic tales. Nahman was the great-grandson of Rabbi Israel, also known as the Baal Shem Tov (Master of the Good Name). With such lineage, people assumed Nahman would follow in the footsteps of the Baal Shem Tov, whose joyous faith gave rise to the Hasidic movement. But the mantle of leadership did not come easily to him. His great-grandfather had taught that God is everywhere and in everything, that God pervades all of nature and is always close to us, if we are aware.

But Nahman did not find easy access to God. Often he felt God's absence even when he focused mind and heart to pray. After he became a rabbi, and disciples came to him for spiritual guidance, Nahman's own inner life continued to be an emotional roller coaster. At times he was overwhelmed by God's nearness, but at other times he felt a vast unbridgeable chasm between himself and God.

In his insightful biography Arthur Green writes that for Nahman:

> The experience of the absence of God, or man's inability to experience God directly, must be taken seriously. Man lives in a world where God cannot be 'seen'; given this reality, doubt is an inevitable part of the life of every religious human being, and the denial of God's very existence is something at which the faithful cannot afford to scoff. [1]

Nahman's life was filled with suffering. Physically weak, he fell prey to a variety of ailments, including tuberculosis. He was prone to bouts of depression. When his two sons died in infancy and his wife succumbed to a chronic illness, Nahman grieved inconsolably. His faith was constantly tested.

Even as he struggled with faith, he was able to reject despair. He transformed God's seeming absence into a spiritual quest. Arthur Green explains, "Faith must be nurtured by constant growth, growth can take place only in the face of challenge, and challenge can exist only in confrontation with the seeming absence of God."[2] Sometimes Nahman failed to convince himself. Yet this man, whose faith was punctuated by periods of anguished doubt, left a legacy of religious parables and sayings that brought comfort to many in his generation and our own as well.

One of the famous sayings of Rabbi Nahman is, "The entire world is a narrow bridge, but the main thing is not to be afraid." This saying was set to music and is still sung in Hasidic circles today. One of my close friends told me about her experience with this song. Nancy is a university professor who teaches political science. Our friendship began when one of our daughters, who was in Nancy's class, made a point of introducing her to us. My wife and I instantly admired her for her love of life, her thirst for knowledge, and her deep concern for others. Her buoyant personality stood in contrast to her ongoing struggle with a progressive, irreversible hearing loss. She lip-reads exceedingly well, appreciates those who speak slowly in her presence, and is especially grateful for the invention of e-mail.

Several years ago Nancy wrote to us when she discovered that she had breast cancer and would shortly be facing surgery and chemotherapy. Nancy wrote, "It is a large experience that has us all a little awed. . . . Some lines of a song have been going through my head." Then she quoted the words of Rabbi Nahman, "The main thing is not to be afraid." Like Rabbi Nahman, Nancy chose to counter her fears with resilience and faith.

I encountered Rabbi Nahman's song again in another surprising context. While on a tour of Central Europe, I attended Sabbath services at a synagogue in Vienna. The congregation consisted of Holocaust survivors, Viennese Jews who had survived the war as well as Jews from other parts of Europe who settled in Vienna afterward. One woman we met at services named Hilda explained to us that unlike other members of the congregation, she survived the war without ever leaving Vienna. Her mother was Jewish, her father Christian. When the authorities discovered her father had married and was living with a non-Aryan, they sent him to a labor camp, where he perished. Hilda and her mother were also arrested and scheduled to be herded onto a train bound for Auschwitz. Miraculously, a glitch in the railroad network delayed the train's departure just long enough for the Allied Forces to liberate the city. She survived to become part of a post-Holocaust Jewish community in Austria.

Hilda concluded her story just as the worship service was about to begin. The rabbi, himself the son of Holocaust survivors, began by humming a melody I immediately recognized. It was the melody composed to accompany the Rabbi Nahman song. Soon the congregation joined in with the words, "The entire world is a narrow bridge, but the main thing is not to be afraid." A shiver went down my spine as I listened to their voices singing the song that could well have been the anthem of this congregation of survivors.

We experience a crisis of faith when, in the midst of God's hiddenness, we find no satisfactory answer to the question, "If God is real and cares for us, why do terrible things happen to good people?" Earlier, I suggested two kinds of answers, based on biblical and rabbinic sources. The first declares that God is all-powerful and all-knowing, that everything proceeds from God. Lacking a "God's eye" perspective, human beings cannot fully understand God's ways. This is the theology that emerges from the book of Job, that says we must trust, or at least accept, that God's purposes are somehow being served in spite of undeserved pain and suffering. Moreover, the rabbinic sages suggest that when we are hurting or confused, we need most to turn toward, not away from, the Source of our being for support.

A second answer that runs concurrently through these texts addresses the question of undeserved suffering quite differently. This view envisions a God of infinite power who is self-limited by choice. God chose to create a world where human beings are free even to disobey God, and where nature is governed by dependable laws. In this view, God does not cause our darker times, but rather weeps with us when we make choices that are destructive to ourselves or others or natural (and unnatural) disasters claim lives. According to this story, God cannot prevent all suffering. It is the price we (and God) pay for divine self-limitation and human freedom. But we may discover, like the biblical Jacob, that God is even in this place and we did not know it. From God comes the courage and strength to cope with life's darker side and the hope that God's love and justice will ultimately prevail.

I have personally lived the tension between these two stories. Neither alone fully satisfies my quest for faith. Rabbi Hanina offers the most extreme statement of the unlimited God story when he says that "a man does not bruise a finger unless it is decreed from above."[3] Another Rabbi Hanina offers this formulation of the self-limited God story, "All is in the hands of Heaven except the fear of Heaven."[4]

Either of these theological views requires an act of faith. If God is in complete control, we have to accept the mystery of suffering and trust that there will be some beneficent end. And if God is self-limited by the world that God chose to create, we must believe that living in such a world is worth its price. When nature's laws produce tornadoes and earthquakes or when humans use their freedom to cause harm to others, we may be unable to declare that life is worth its price. This is precisely the issue we struggle with in our pursuit of faith.

At certain times in my life, I frankly did not find much solace in either story or explanation. Standing at the grave of Nicholas, the seven-year-old child killed in a freak accident, my own faith ebbed to the point of nonexistence. God's hiddenness at that moment seemed to me the equivalent of

God's unreality. In the presence of his parents, Jack and Linda, I recited the appropriate prayers including the words, "Praised be thou, O God, whose judgments are true," but my heart was not in it. I understood completely when Jack told our congregation that in the days following Nicholas's death his recitation of the Kaddish, which proclaims trust in God, was an empty exercise, and the worship services he dutifully attended "were gray and meaningless."

But Jack did not give up on God. He continued to pray and in time the prayers became more meaningful to him. I watched in the months that followed as God's healing presence helped sustain him and Linda. They did not give up on life and found the strength to go on.

In such terribly troubling moments when my faith has left me, I too have not abandoned my quest for God or my need of prayer. As difficult as it is sometimes to live with God, I have not found it possible to live without God. Fortunately, those moments of spiritual crisis have been superseded by other times when I have experienced signs of God's power and love in my life and the lives of others.

Jeremiah has always been my favorite of the biblical prophets because he is so human and so vocal about his spiritual crises. My partiality for Jeremiah also has something to do with Sheldon Blank, my Bible professor at the Hebrew Union College seminary. Ordinarily a mild-mannered and soft-spoken man, Professor Blank underwent a complete metamorphosis when he taught the book of Jeremiah. Taking on the personality of the emotional prophet, he seemed to become Jeremiah reincarnate in our classroom. There is something in the poignancy and passion of Jeremiah that touches us all.

In Jeremiah's confessions, we get a searing glimpse of the prophet's inner struggle. Jeremiah had been called by God for a prophetic life that brought him nothing but anguish. He urged Israel to repent and change its ways on the eve of the imminent Babylonian invasion that resulted in the first exile of the Israelites from their homeland. When Jeremiah prophesied that the kingdom of Judah would fall because of its own internal moral corruption, his friends and family turned against him. When he challenged King Zedekiah in God's name, the king imprisoned him. Friendless and desolate, Jeremiah turned his anger and despair against the God who had commissioned him to deliver this unwelcome message. In passages of deep personal anguish, he laments his calling as a prophet:

> Woe is me, my mother, that you ever bore me—
> A man of conflict and strife with all the land!
> I have not lent,
> And I have not borrowed;
> Yet everyone curses me. . . .
> O LORD, you know—
>
> Remember me and take thought of me,
> Avenge me on those who persecute me;
> Do not yield to Your patience,
> Do not let me perish!
> Consider how I have borne insult
> On Your account. . . .
> I have not sat in the company of revelers
> And made merry!
> I have sat lonely because of Your hand upon me,
> For You have filled me with gloom.
> Why must my pain be endless,
> My wound incurable,
> Resistant to healing?
> You have been to me like a spring that fails,
> Like waters that cannot be relied on.
>   (Jeremiah 15:10, 15-18)

Jeremiah poured out his bitterness to God and waited for an answer. In the depths of his soul, he heard a reply:

If you produce what is noble
Out of the worthless,
You shall be My spokesman.
They shall come back to you,
Not you to them.
Against this people I will make you
As a fortified wall of bronze:
They will attack you,
But they shall not overcome you,
For I am with you to deliver and save you.
(Jeremiah 15:19-20) [5]

In the course of his prayer, Jeremiah comes to understand that there is a price for serving God in this world. He cannot refrain from speaking out the truth even though it has cost him dearly. "They shall come back to you, / Not you to them," God tells him. Above all, Jeremiah finds strength in his renewed sense of God's nearness and support.

Jeremiah's confessions are uncensored prayers that expressed anger, resentment, feelings of abandonment, and self-pity. But through prayer, Jeremiah experienced a divine response that moved him from despair to a more sturdy faith in the validity of his vocation.

The Hebrew Bible contains many examples of what we call confrontational prayer. Abraham argued with God over the fate of the innocent persons in Sodom. Abraham dared to ask God, "Will the judge of all the earth not act justly?"

The book of Job is also a classic example of confrontational prayer. Job refuses to believe that he deserves the bad things that happened to him, from the loss of his wealth, to the death of members of his family, to the illness that ravaged his body. Angrily Job confronts God:

Remove your hand from me,
And let not Your terror frighten me.
Then summon me and I will respond,

Or I will speak and You reply to me. . . .
Advise me of my transgression and sin.
Why do You hide Your face,
And treat me like an enemy? (Job 13:21-24)

Out of this struggle, Job is reassured by God that he does not deserve his misfortunes and is not being punished for any transgression. Job comes to terms with a God whose ways are beyond his understanding. He lives in the presence of mystery and trusts that beyond it, there is meaning.

The ancient rabbis had a name for the confrontational prayers of Abraham, Jeremiah, and Job. They called them *chutzpah k'lapay shemaya*, which may be translated as "defiant boldness in God's presence." In their moments of spiritual crisis, the rabbinic sages also addressed prayers to God that sound more like challenges. When the Roman Emperor brutally oppressed the Jews of Judea, Rabbi Ishmael changed the wording of a standard Jewish prayer. The original prayer was based on "The Song at the Sea," a prayer of praise led by Miriam and Moses upon crossing the Red Sea. When the Israelites were delivered by God from Egyptian bondage, they proclaimed, "Who is like you among the gods, O Lord . . . [who] will reign forever and ever."[6]

In his anguish at the Roman atrocities and God's apparent silence, Rabbi Ishmael changed the text of the prayer. Instead of reading, "Who is like you among the gods *(elim)*?" he changed the prayer to read, "Who is like you among the 'silent ones' *(illemim)*, able to listen to the torments and insults of the evil man [Titus] and remain still [or mute]?" By this play on words Rabbi Ishmael changed a prayer of praise into a confrontational prayer rebuking God.[7]

The problem of God's apparent silence in the presence of ruthless evil is by no means confined to ancient times. God's silence in the time of the Nazis has triggered both crises of faith and confrontational prayer. Elie Wiesel has used this confrontational mode of dealing with anguish and the lapse of faith in several of his novels. In *The Gates of the Forest*, a young man named Gregor survives the war posing as a deaf-mute peasant before linking up with other Jews in the resistance. At the war's end, having lost everyone he loved, Gregor is obsessed with the question, *Where was God?* Gregor winds up in Brooklyn, where he frequents a Hasidic congregation, not to pray, but to challenge the rabbi about his ability to pray to a silent God. "Do you want me to stop praying and start shouting?" the rabbi asks him. "Yes," whispered Gregor.

During their impassioned debate, Gregor suddenly realizes that he no longer wants to win this argument. The rabbi answers him:

> Who says that power comes from a shout, an outcry rather than from a prayer? From anger rather than compassion? Where do you find certainties when you claim to have denied them? The man who goes singing to death is the brother of the man who goes to death fighting. A song on the lips is worth a dagger in the hand. I take this song and make it mine.[8]

When Gregor himself is finally able to pray, he does so as an act of defiance; he says the Kaddish both to affirm his own existence and bear witness to the lives of the people who were killed. His healing begins when he can once more speak to a living God, even if in anger.

Wiesel's characters are challengers of God in a world where God is silent, but they challenge God because they need to believe in him. Confrontational prayer reveals a great paradox. The anger and bitter defiance often reflect a deep-seated yearning for the rekindling of faith. A Yiddish proverb declares, "If God had a house, all its windows would be broken." This statement expresses a curious blend of angry confrontation and intimacy. Think of a moment of exasperation when a child will exclaim to a parent, "I hate you! You don't love me." What is the child seeking to convey? "I need to believe you love me! Please show me that you do." Confrontation in an adult relationship may signal, "I care enough to struggle with you. If I didn't care, I would just walk away." The great confrontations between God and Jeremiah, and other figures down through the ages, all bespeak a yearning for faith. In each case, the protestor is not struck down. God is not alienated by confrontational prayer and the relationship is sometimes stronger after the encounter.

Some years ago Rabbi Gerald Wolpe experienced a crisis of faith when his wife suffered a debilitating stroke. During a High Holiday service, he shared his personal anguish with his congregation, crying out, "God where are you? God I do not always understand. . . . Why have You allowed this to happen to her?"

The following year in his Rosh Hashanah sermon, Rabbi Wolpe related how his confrontational prayer of the previous year helped him survive as a believing Jew. He recalled, "I felt the searing power of *Avinu Malkenu* [a prayer that begins, "Our Father, Our King . . . "] when with all my heart I cried, 'God, be good and save me, I cannot do it by myself.' "[9] Then he quoted the words of the French poet Appolinaire, in whose poem people are reluctant to come to the edge. God pushes them and they fly.

Reflecting upon the year that had passed, he observed, "I walked, I moved, I survived, I remained human. He pushed me, but I learned how to fly." His wife's disability challenged him to the limits; a year later, he was grateful that he could meet that challenge.

Aaron is a sweet, sensitive young man in his early twenties. I met him at the local community center and shortly afterwards, he came to see me. He wanted to talk about his personal battle against drug addiction. He said he was clean for fifteen months and felt better than he had in a long time.

For many years, Aaron told me, religion was not a big factor in his life. He didn't find it meaningful to pray because he wasn't sure he believed in God. As part of his treatment, he agreed to attend a private rehab center. At one group therapy session, each of the young people in the group was asked to openly express personal anger at someone as if he or she were there listening. Virtually everyone who spoke before him that day directed their anger at their parents. When it was his turn, much to his surprise, Aaron exclaimed, "I blame God."

Aaron accused God of saddling him with an unkind fate. He was born with a birth defect that did not impair him physically or mentally, but made him very self-conscious. His childhood and adolescence were very unhappy; at school he was withdrawn and shy. In college, he took refuge in drugs. Now in the presence of his wounded peers, Aaron accused God of dealing him an oppressive handicap. He vented his resentment with deep bitterness and tears.

After his outburst of anger, Aaron felt God was closer to him than ever before. Since that day, he has made regular time for meditation and prayer. He acknowledged his dependence, his neediness, and his gratitude to a power greater than himself for giving him the strength to overcome his addiction.

The American philosopher Alfred North Whitehead described religious experience at its profoundest level as the transition "from God the void to God the enemy, and from God the enemy to God the companion."[10] Prayer can help us make that journey. Prayers of angry engagement and desperate cries for help may yield again to the prayers of awe and gratitude. Such was the case for Rabbi Wolpe, and for my young friend Aaron.

If we can persist beyond numbness, anger, and bewilderment, we too may find a deeper faith on the other side of the abyss. Over the years many who have made this journey will say, "I have never felt closer to God than now."

This is not to suggest that once we have undergone a crisis and moved beyond it we will forever be spared the struggle for faith. In even the best marriage, periods of glowing intimacy and deep gratitude are punctuated by moments of nagging doubt and estrangement when the words "I love you" do not come spontaneously to our lips. So there will be periods when the praise of God bursts from our soul and other moments when our covenant must be sustained by memories of better times and the hope that present trials will soon pass.

The mature believer, like the mature lover, must take the long view, expect some difficult challenges, and be all the more appreciative of times of wholeness and well-being. Once we have weathered a religious crisis we realize there is enough pain and sorrow in this world to arm the agnostic or atheist. Our relationship with God is at best a covenant with hidden clauses, namely, the unexpected events in life. We must ultimately decide if we believe we are alone or if there is a God who cares for us.

The rabbinic sages asked, looking back at our biblical forebears, how did Abraham resolve his crises of faith? Rabbi Isaac responded with this *Aggadah,* Abraham may be compared to a man who was traveling from place to place when he saw a palace radiantly illuminated. The man thought, "Is it possible there is no one who cares for this palace?" Then someone appeared to him and said, "I am the owner of this palace." So it was that whenever Abraham saw a world that was radiantly illuminated he asked, "Is it conceivable that the world is without a guide?"[11]

Rabbi Abraham Joshua Heschel adds a twentieth-century gloss to this parable. He notes that the Hebrew phrase *birah doleket* can be translated as "a palace full of light" but can also mean "a palace in flames." Is the palace radiantly illuminated or consumed in flames? The ambiguity of those Hebrew words reveals another dimension to the parable. Abraham came to the awareness of God's reality when the world seemed full of radiant light but he also believed in God when the world seemed to be consumed in flames. In the first instance he asked, "There is so much radiance in the world, is it conceivable the world is without a giver of light?" And in the latter circumstances he asked, "the world is engulfed in flames. . . . Is it possible there is no Lord to take this misfortune to heart?"[12]

Sometimes the world is so awesomely beautiful to us we cannot imagine there is no creator responsible for it. And there are other times when the world seems so drenched in violence and evil that we ask, "Is there no God to care how we live our lives?" Of all the possible answers to that question, faith remains the most life-affirming response to the glory and pathos of being human.

Earlier we noted the climactic meeting of the long estranged brothers, Jacob and Esau. When Jacob heard his brother and a band of four hundred armed men were approaching his camp, Jacob feared that his aggrieved brother was coming to avenge the loss of the birthright. In response to an imminent threat, Jacob divided his camp and sent his family on to the other side of the river. He sent messengers ahead with gifts to assuage Esau's wrath while he prayed for divine deliverance. The biblical text describes his night of anxious waiting:

Jacob was left alone. A man wrestled him until the break of dawn. When he saw that he had not prevailed against him, he wrenched Jacob's hip at its socket, so that the socket of his hip was strained. . . . Then he [the man] said, "Let me go, for dawn is breaking." But he answered, "I will not let you go, unless you bless me." Said the other, "What is your name?" He replied, "Jacob." Said he, "Your name shall no longer be Jacob, but Israel, for you have striven with beings divine and human, and have prevailed." (Genesis 32:25-29)

Perhaps this story is the Bible's most powerful image for the confrontational dimension of our relationship to God, and for our struggle for faith as well. Like Jacob, we are all "God-wrestlers." But like Jacob, we too may emerge from our struggles bruised but blessed and ready to face the challenges of life with the assurance that we are not alone.

Chapter 7

When Prayer Is Not Enough

The prisoner cannot free himself. —Talmud, Berakoth 5b

A STORY IN THE TALMUD tells of a time when Rabbi Yohanan fell ill. Rabbi Hanina visited him and asked, "Are your sufferings cherished by you?" Rabbi Yohanan replied, "Neither they nor the reward for them." Whereupon Rabbi Hanina said to his friend, "Give me your hand." Yohanan gave him his hand, and Hanina raised him up from the sickbed. Was this a healing of the spirit or body or both? We do not know. To the question, "Why could not Rabbi Yohanan heal himself?" the Talmud simply responds, "The prisoner cannot free himself."[1]

When we confront physical or emotional illness, we are not always in a position to heal ourselves. Such is the case even if the "prisoner" is a rabbi, presumably adept at the discipline of prayer.

This story also teaches us that prayer, even confrontational prayer—for all its power and efficacy, may not be a sufficient response to a troubled situation. Jacob discovered that God may be present at those moments when we are totally bereft of human support. ("God is even in this place and I did not know it.") Later, however, Jacob encountered a loving, embracing Esau, and knew this experience too was "like seeing the face of God." The helpful presence of another person often mediates God's presence. This also was true for the troubled Yohanan, when he encountered Rabbi Hanina.

Rabbi Nahman of Bratslav, who in times of crisis affirmed the bridging power of prayer, also believed in the healing power of words we speak to another person. Two centuries before Freud, Nahman taught that if we talk out our pain and tell our story to a trusted other, we may better exorcise the demons that torment our souls.

Rabbi Hanina and Rabbi Nahman were spiritual healers. We live in an age of biomedical technology and psychotherapy. Has religion's role been completely preempted by the therapies of our age? I do not think so. The best among clergy, physicians, and psychotherapists appreciate the complementary healing roles of each.

When I counsel people and it becomes obvious their capacity for intimacy has been severely impaired by earlier life experiences, I will defer to the psychotherapist to help them explore those blockages. As far as I am concerned, that therapist is mediating the healing power of God.

There are, I suspect, some clergy who refuse to acknowledge the legitimate role of psychotherapy. But then I know a few psychotherapists who do not appreciate the healing power of religious counseling. Freud himself dismissed religious sentiment as a sign of lingering immaturity. I recall the story of the therapist who decided his patient had reached the termination of her therapy, but when she expressed renewed interest in her religion, the therapist murmured, "Looks like we've got more work to do."

Carl Jung, a disciple who broke with Freud, took a different view of the healing power of religion. Jung once wrote:

> Among all my patients in the second half of life—that is to say, over thirty-five—there has not been one whose problem

in the last resort was not that of finding a religious outlook on life. It is safe to say that every one of them fell ill because he had lost what the living religions of every age have given to their followers, and none of them has been really healed who did not regain his religious outlook.[2]

Jung suggests his services are necessary only because secular men and women have lost the spiritual support of traditional religion in facing existential situations. Jung's claims seem to me as excessive as Freud's. It is possible to be spiritually well grounded and still benefit from psychotherapy.

Happily, many contemporary therapists and clergy appreciate the power and limits of their respective systems and recognize the need for a healing partnership. Dr. Lauren Artress likes the metaphor used by Dr. Ruth Tiffani Barnhouse of "the spiritual director being the music teacher and the psychotherapist being the piano tuner. A psychotherapist helps to fix the ego, helps it to be healthier. A spiritual director teaches us how to play the right notes—teaching a tune from the music of life."[3]

I was a young rabbi, in my first solo position after having served two years as assistant rabbi in Hartford. I came to my position in Flint, Michigan, when I was not yet twenty-eight years old. I was married only a year and my wife, Joan, was eight months pregnant. During those two years, two of our three daughters were born. Certainly, mine was a productive rabbinate.

To the outside world I was quite successful. Young couples were drawn into the congregation. My adult education classes and life cycle observances and preaching were generally well received. I was active in the larger community and my representations seemed to evoke pride in the members of my community. Congregants paid me the strange compliment of saying, "You'll not be here long; you're too good."

Internally, I was plagued by deep anxiety and realized I was battling depression. I perceived anything less than total involvement in the temple by my contemporaries or elders as a sign of my personal failure. I felt more fear of failure than any excitement or creativity as I prepared or delivered my sermons. I found any social gatherings with our friends more a threatening chore than a pleasure.

I recall sitting at the table and nibbling at food that I once savored and devoured, aware that I had lost my appetite. I was drained of any desire for sexual intimacy with my wife and could not really enjoy playing with my infant daughter. When Joan announced that she was pregnant with our second child, I was more panicked than pleased. Those many months must surely rank as the low point in my adult life.

I responded to the crisis in two ways. After some toughing it out and praying that my depression would pass, I overcame my reluctance to acknowledge that "the prisoner cannot free himself." I was fortunate to find a wonderful psychotherapist. The healing I received in those many therapy hours that explored my early childhood experiences and relationship to my parents, though not without pain, came to be regarded as instances of God's redeeming love. And yes, my therapist became for me an angel, a messenger of God at a crucial time in my life.

Simultaneously, I struggled to listen—to really listen to those religious stories that infused my preaching and teaching. I suppose one could say I tried to practice what I preached. Under the best of circumstances, I would have combined my psychotherapy with a visit to my rabbi for this kind of spiritual counsel. Unfortunately, there wasn't a rabbi in my community with whom I felt comfortable sharing my inner anguish.

At one point, when I was well into psychotherapy, the validity of those stories for my life attained the clarity of a fresh revelation. I remember scribbling on a scrap of paper the words that leaped from my mind to pen faster than I could write them, "I am of worth even though sometimes I mess up or fail, because I am created in the image of God. I have tasks to do. I should focus, not on whether I will succeed or fail, but on doing the task I am intended to do with all my heart, as an offering to my Creator. I must believe that if I do all I can, God, the redeemer and helper, will somehow sustain me."

In that crisis, and in subsequent years, I have had reason to believe that the wisdom of my faith and its stories were as healing and at least as important as psychotherapy. The notes I scribbled many years ago and placed in my wallet became too tattered to preserve anymore but the message remains indelibly with me.

People who act as healers receive training in a body of knowledge to help them understand and respond appropriately to the human condition. My physician friends have spent years in medical school to master the cumulative medical tradition on body systems, diseases, and therapies. My psychiatrist friends have studied medical and psychological theories. So armed, they apply their tools to diagnose and treat emotional illness.

What about clergy? What are the resources of my trade as I counsel people and try to help them? Of course, my response to the pain of another is the human response: I must assure them of my empathy and caring. But when I offer spiritual counsel to others, I am both a listener and a teller of stories. My most valuable resource is *Aggadah*—the primary religious stories found in the Bible and elaborated upon by the sages of the Talmud. These stories address life's deepest questions: *Who am I? What is my life task? What can I hope for?* These stories speak of God as creator, guide, helper.

They embody the perspective that life has some transcendent order and purpose. They confirm life's meaning even in the midst of suffering and death.

Through these stories my own life is invested with its deepest source of value, direction, and hope. They provide a lens for experiencing God in my life and have shaped my counseling with people who struggle for meaning in a broken world.

The very first story in Genesis speaks of God as Creator. In my prayers each morning I am instructed to say, "Praised are you, O God, who renews daily the work of creation," and the very first prayer is, "I thank you, God, for having restored my soul to me this day in your graciousness; how great is your faithfulness." God is the Source of my being.

Not only our existence but our essential worth derives from God. We are created *b'tzelem elohim,* "in the image of God." Rabbi Abraham Joshua Heschel once explained that we are forbidden to make an image of God; that is idolatry. Yet, paradoxically, each person is an image of God. The divine is reflected within each of us. None of us may act as if we were God and no person should be worshiped as if he or she were God. Only God is God. But the divine is imprinted in each of us. Hence, in the words of a modern meditation, "Each of our lives is worth the life of the whole world; in each one is the breath of the Ultimate One."[4]

Therefore, we are worth more than the chemicals in our bodies, more than our services or talents can command in the marketplace, more than the sum of our good deeds, more than the number of people who like us, more than the place or no place ascribed to us in the social register. Our intrinsic worth derives most fundamentally not from what we do but from who we are: We are children of God.

From the creation story we also learn the human being's place in the world. God takes special notice of Adam and Eve and has special expectations of them. The unique covenant between us and God also confers special dignity and honor. Even when we are most aware of our failures we are reminded of our covenantal status. On Yom Kippur in the midst of confessing our sins we declare, "What are we, what is our life, what our righteousness, what our virtue, what our power, what our heroism? [but] from the beginning you have distinguished the human beings and empowered them to stand before you."

From this it follows that even when we stumble and fall, the God who judges us and holds us to account also loves us unconditionally. Another prayer, also from the High Holiday liturgy, reminds us "We are your beloved / you are our friend." I am always deeply moved by that prayer that we recite on the very day we acknowledge and atone for our sins. Those words, though spoken in the context of Israel's particular covenant with God, are the ground of Judaism's understanding of God's universal covenant with humankind, even as the Christian understanding of God's universal love derives from the figure of Jesus.

All of which leads to a fundamental truth: God loves us and therefore we are of precious worth even when we are inclined not to love or value ourselves. At such times it is especially important to remember that we are loved and cherished by the One who created us so that we may value ourselves enough to make changes in the way we live.

In that same Genesis narrative, God calls Adam and Eve to responsibility. They discover their power to serve or betray God. After eating from the forbidden tree, they hide and God calls, "Where are you?"

Rabbi Shneur Zalman of Ladi was the founder of a branch of Hasidism that later came to be known as Lubavitch or Chabad. When the rabbi spent time in a czarist prison, his atheist guard taunted him with this challenge, "If your God is supposed to be omniscient, why did God have to ask Adam, 'Where are you?' " The rabbi replied, "God called Adam as God calls to each of us mortal creatures, 'Where are you in your world?' It is as if God says, 'You have lived forty-six years and what have you done with the limited time you have been given?' " Hearing his own age mentioned, the warden trembled.⁵

The second core narrative of the Hebrew Bible—the Sinai story—reveals the way we are intended to live. The God who calls us into being commands us to walk on one path rather than another. Before doing a religious deed *(mitzvah)*, a Jew is expected to recite, "Praised are you, O God, ruling spirit of the universe, who has sanctified us [who has made our lives significant] by giving us deeds to do in response to your will."

The story of the giving of the Law at Sinai also defines an attitude toward time. Time is an awareness of our mortality. That awareness is what caused the warden to tremble. We cannot conquer time but we may sanctify it. We can make our time significant.

Faith does not enable me to elude the ravages of aging or the angel of death. I have no power to transcend time but I am able to answer for the time that is mine. And there is a divine intention for our lives. God calls to every one of us, "Where are you?" As God called to Noah, "Walk with integrity." And to Abraham, "Be a blessing." And to Moses and to Israel, "You shall be holy."

To answer for the time God has given us, to act as God's faithful partner in this world—that is the meaning of God's call to Adam, to Abraham, to Moses at Sinai, and to each of us. God has special deeds for each of us to do in this world. By doing them we help repair that tiny corner of God's world entrusted to us. We fulfill the meaning of our lives and become a blessing.

Finally there is the exodus story. It speaks of God as helper, savior, redeemer. God brought us out of Egypt and continues to liberate us from the seemingly hopeless circumstances of our lives. Nobel laureate Joseph Brodsky once said that the purpose of literature is "to show a man at the end of his wits an opening, a pattern to follow." Unintentionally, Brodsky also described the meaning of faith.

There are times when I have felt trapped by the circumstances of my life: no exit, no solution, no escape. I have feared the worst only to discover much to my amazement and gratitude that alternatives appeared. At times in my life when I have been close to despair and seriously wondered if life was worth the trouble I have often been surprised by a touch of grace. Sometimes it comes as an amazing renewal of my power just to carry on. At such times, I become newly aware of the presence of a God who is my helper and redeemer.

These narratives that affirm God as creator, giver of Torah, and redeemer are the primary stories for the reading of our lives. God created me in the divine image. (I am precious to God. I am of infinite worth.) God has given me the Torah. (There is a way I am intended to live, tasks I am intended to do.) God frees me from the Egypts of my life. (God is with me as helper and redeemer.)

Telling these stories in one form or another and relating them to our lives is what preaching, teaching, and spiritual counseling are all about. There are teachable moments when needful persons make precious connections between *Aggadah,* the story line of faith, and their individual lives. The role of a religious counselor is to help people make such connections.

At the time I met with her, Melissa insisted on seeing me that very day, if possible. She was fresh out of college and about to begin her first job. There was a quiver in her voice. When she sat in my office she said she had decided to accept a position with a mortgage banking firm rather than enter law school. She was excited and scared. What if she didn't measure up? Actually her track record was good. As a teenager she was already labeled a "superachiever," but the fear of failure and the uncertainty generated by each new test of her powers filled her with great anxiety.

In earlier years, I would have felt my mission accomplished by simply referring her to a psychotherapist under whose guidance she could probe and exorcise fears stemming from earlier relationships not fully understood. I still believe, of course, that psychotherapy can be helpful, but Freud himself said that the purpose of therapy was to help transform "neurotic misery into normal unhappiness." What of the *normal* fears, uncertainties, and unhappiness of life?

At first glance, the problem presented by Melissa may not seem weighty enough to illustrate the power and importance of a religious perspective on human life. She was afraid of failing as a mortgage banker and yearned to pursue her career with less performance anxiety. Listening to her, I remembered some of the fears and anxieties of my younger self on my first "real" job.

The fact is Melissa came to me because I was a rabbi. Her "presenting" issue was really a transparent window exposing the most existential of human concerns: *Is there anything in my religion to help me cope with my fears?*

A psychotherapist may have focused on the roots of her anxiety and fear of failure; I decided a different perspective on facing life's challenges would help her more. Melissa needed to accept herself on a learning curve; of course, she would make mistakes in the process, but she had to separate them from her worth and value as a person. "If God is the Source of your being and the ultimate Source of your value," I explained, "then your worth does not depend on what you do or how well you succeed in any of life's tasks. You have an inalienable dignity, you are precious even should you fail. You are created in the image of God. In the profoundest sense, your worth is not dictated by how many clients you attract, or what deals you clinch, or what bonus you earn; your essential value is rooted not in what you do but in who you are: You are a person in whom there is the spark of the divine."

The key is, I told her, not to be obsessed by whether she succeeded or failed. She would find herself much less fearful of failure if she focused on doing her task with all her might, and doing it not so much as an ego trip to prove her worth, but as her small offering to God in that portion of the world entrusted to her care. She seemed visibly to relax when I urged her to trust God in finding her way and to have patience and compassion for herself.

The very process of psychotherapy may illuminate the distinction between what we need from the psychotherapist and what we need from someone who speaks from a religious perspective. Rabbi Eugene Borowitz once explored that tension in a lecture to health care professionals at the Texas Medical Center's Institute of Religion. He explained that we learn at an early age the importance of pleasing others. We can become so programmed automatically to respond to what others want of us that we lose a sense of what we feel or want for ourselves.

Here the psychotherapist can be especially helpful. The therapist is a nonjudgmental nurturer and listener. In time we may be able to say things that we have not been able to say to others or even admit to ourselves.

People in therapy can be hard to live with. They may begin asserting themselves or, seemingly, overasserting themselves. But in time, Rabbi Borowitz concluded, they must reconsider not only their needs with which they are now in touch, but the needs of others. They must redraw the balance between self-love and love of others, between preoccupation with self-fulfillment and responsibility to the people in their lives. Here is where religious teachings come into play.

A much quoted saying by Rabbi Hillel asks a rhetorical question, "If I am not for myself, who will be for me?" But the second line is equally important, "If I am only for myself, what am I?"[6] What kind of living gives meaning to my life? How do I live with integrity? Religion cannot take the place of psychotherapy, but psychotherapy cannot take the place of religion in asking these kinds of questions.

Consider, for example, the human problem of guilt. One of the goals of psychotherapy is to help free us from irrational guilt feelings, those distorted images that derive from formative experiences with the primary figures in our lives. But religion helps us face the real guilt that results from our own actions. There are things we *should* feel guilty about! For such acts, the answer is not psychotherapy but confession, repentance, and an opening of self to the forgiving love of God. The Jewish High Holy Day season, with its magnificent rituals of confession, contrition, and forgiveness cannot be replaced by a month or a year on a psychiatrist's couch. The religious process of repentance can also be a powerful incentive for changing the way we think and act.

Rabbi Harlan J. Wechsler tells of a man who had to appear in court for a charge of embezzlement. He intended to plead guilty. When the man came to see Rabbi Wechsler, the rabbi asked, "Why did you come to see a rabbi? . . . You will pay a penalty. You will be punished according to the law.

Won't that make you feel better?" The man replied, "There is something higher. . . . My life has been corrupted; God knows!"[7]

For real guilt we may need to acknowledge accountability to a higher reality and follow the traditional religious path to spiritual wholeness. We often speak of the need to forgive ourselves. The message of religious faith is that we are truly able to forgive ourselves only because the God to whom we are accountable forgives. But the notion of divine forgiveness also commits us to making changes in the way we live.

Michael is a successful real estate agent who was referred to me by his therapist. At our first meeting Michael said he was in my office only because his therapist had told him to come. He then told me his story. He had been married for almost ten years and had two young children, aged four and seven. His wife, in his own words, was "a good mother and homemaker."

In recent years, however, Michael had become increasingly interested in his spiritual life and had explored his interest in religion through courses, retreats, and study groups. His wife tolerated his participation in these activities but did not really share his interest and felt threatened by it as well. It became one of many things they could no longer discuss.

Michael then described an encounter with one of his clients, a recent divorcée, whose home he was trying to sell. He discovered he had a great deal in common with this woman, who was also sympathetic to his marital distress. He found himself visiting her more frequently than their professional relationship required. Michael felt a profound kinship with this woman, who was struggling with the aftermath of her own failed marriage, and eventually there was a physical relationship as well.

Michael continued to live with his wife while visiting this woman for periodic rendezvous. He was feeling bad about the deception, so he told his wife. He promised to end the affair but didn't, which caused a painful contradiction between his spiritual track and his actions. In the meantime, the other woman, who had come to depend on him for emotional support, was waiting for him to leave his wife.

I asked Michael what the psychotherapist had said about all of this. He responded, "He doesn't speak or judge, he listens and asks questions." Apparently, his therapist was helping him to sort out his own needs and feelings of unhappiness. They rarely talked about the needs of his wife and family, or the other woman waiting for him to make a decision. Meanwhile, his conscience gnawed at him. That day I asked Michael if he felt he had violated the terms of his covenant with God. With tears in his eyes, he responded, "Yes." I suggested that if he wanted to be authentic in his spiritual journey why not break off the relationship with the other woman and devote himself fully to the therapy? Was he making a good faith effort to save the marriage? After all their years together, didn't he owe that to his wife and children?

After hearing my words Michael said, "I know why I needed to come to you. You are telling me what I know is true. My therapist helps me understand my psyche, you help me understand my soul."

Two months later Michael made an appointment to see me for an update. He said things were not good. He was in therapy with his wife and realized that the marriage had ended years earlier when they began having problems and did not address them. He tried to quit the affair, but when the other woman called at his office, he wanted to speak to her and they continued to meet. The deception continued. He had trouble sleeping. He felt a great malaise. But although he prayed for strength to control his impulses, he couldn't seem to give the other woman up and make a real commitment to his marriage.

I told him, "The good news is that you feel lousy, that this betrayal has taken its toll." I concluded that he could make no genuine turning in either direction without some sacrifice, but he was trying to have his cake and eat it too. I described his guilt as a hopeful sign.

I urged him to tell his wife of the deception. If he knew the marriage had ended, then he should move out. I added that he might need to do some grieving himself for the end of the marriage.

Before he left my office that day Michael said, "What you are telling me I need to hear and on some level I want to hear. I do feel ashamed, I want to be a good person and do right by the people in my life. I guess I am scared about the new possibilities. I haven't moved in with this woman yet although she wants me to. I am not ready to make a commitment. I tell her I need time." He then added, "I have started to look for an apartment."

A month later, Michael made another appointment. He told me that following our previous meeting he was moved to act responsibly. He left home. But after a few days in his apartment he felt terribly alone and missed his children. He returned home and shortly thereafter terminated the affair. He continued seeing his therapist, and he and his wife began to see a marriage counselor once a week. "It's hard work and I don't know if we'll succeed," he said. He felt they were working on a new start to their marriage, discussing issues and differences they had always avoided in the past. He hoped they would make it.

I asked him why he kept coming back to me when each time I seemed to add to his disquietude. He replied, "I needed to be seen as you saw me, which was very different from the way my therapist saw me." The psychotherapist focused on the underlying psychological factors that contributed to his present midlife crisis. I focused on his need to restore spiritual integrity by either working wholeheartedly to repair his marriage, or by ending it. There was a moral as well as psychological component to his misery.

As of this writing, I do not know the end of this story but in my sessions with Michael, I felt his therapist and I were playing different but complementary roles in getting him to make decisions and take responsibility for his actions.

At times religious counseling may help a confused and troubled person balance the two parts of Hillel's dictum—to respect ourselves and respect others. Jocelyn and Karl were happily married and enjoyed many of the same things, including a love of classical music. When a medical exam revealed that Karl had an inoperable cancer and that he was expected to live no more than a year, their life was radically changed. Within a month, Karl was confined to his bed at home. Jocelyn took leave from her job in order to be with him almost constantly and literally to nurse him. Fortunately his pain was minimal but his weakness was progressive. Being Karl's caregiver was very wearing for Jocelyn, especially as he was demanding, often sullen, and generally intolerant of her absence from the room, much less the house, for more than a brief interlude.

Jocelyn loved Karl and nursed him tenderly; she understood how much he needed her and much of the time felt good about being there for him at this last stage of his life. After six weeks of absence from work, her supervisor called and told Jocelyn that her employer could not maintain her leave of absence more than a week or so longer. If she could not return to work, her job would be filled by someone else.

At that point, Jocelyn made an appointment to see me after a neighbor agreed to stay with Karl. As she described her dilemma, Jocelyn sobbed openly. She explained that she was grateful for her marriage and their years together, and that she loved Karl and understood his emotional as well as physical dependence on her. She wanted to be there for him. But she was also concerned about her future. She knew that Karl had lived well on his salary but never saved. He had virtually no life insurance and would leave her no monetary resources.

She loved her job and explained how difficult it would be to find another at the same level. Visibly uneasy, she confessed that it had become intolerable to nurse Karl without a break. She was exhausted all the time. She felt guilty about her resentment and was fearful about her own future if she left her job. "Rabbi," she said, "I'm confused and don't know what I should do." As I pressed her, Jocelyn acknowledged that she wanted to provide a caregiver for Karl and return to work, but she feared that doing so would make her hate herself and feel terribly guilty. She felt trapped into continuing the full-time nursing of her husband for the duration of his life.

Jocelyn saw me as a religious authority and she wanted my guidance. She knew that caring for loved ones in need was a religious imperative, but she needed me to remind her of the first part of Hillel's teaching, "If I am not for myself, who will be for me?" She felt surprised but tremendously relieved when I told her that if she were a *tzaddik* (a saint), she could be expected to follow the path of ignoring her own needs and focusing only on those of her husband. But the Torah does not command that we be saints; it expects that we be loving to others without ceasing to love and care for ourselves. Karl had no right to expect her to ignore a concern for herself.

She needed to set boundaries: she would go back to work to preserve her job and find some relief from her round-the-clock nursing at home. She would provide a suitable caregiver for Karl in her absence and be there for him when she was home. If that became a burden that she could not handle alone, she agreed to seek additional help. Under this arrangement, I explained, she would be much less resentful and more able to express the genuine love that she felt for her husband.

Both Michael and Jocelyn needed religious counseling. Both were people of conscience who considered themselves accountable to God for their actions. Neither could find an adequate *moral* response from a psychotherapist. Michael needed guidance to take seriously his malaise, his feeling of guilt, and to act responsibly. Jocelyn needed permission from a religious authority to consider her own needs no less than her husband's. Jocelyn needed to hear, "If I am not for myself, who will be for me?" Michael needed to confront the question, "If I am only for myself, what am I?" None of us lives in isolation; we live in a world with others, and religion reminds us of the balance.

Psychotherapy and religion are not substitutes for each other. Each discipline or system is involved in healing. Each may mediate God's grace for those who seek counsel in time of trouble.

We who offer counsel of one kind or another may become "the face of God" in the lives of others. The Talmud's question, "Why could Rabbi Yohanan not raise himself?" is fundamental and the answer is compelling: "The prisoner cannot free himself." At some point in our lives, we may all need to respond to trouble by seeking human counsel. The psychotherapist helps us tune the instrument that God has given us. Religion gives us the music to play and enables us to discover our place in the concert. And the one who helps us heal the mind, body, and spirit—whether physician, therapist, clergyperson, or friend—is an agent of the Holy One.

Chapter 8

The Power of Love

Love your fellow as yourself: I am the LORD.
—Leviticus 19:18

WORDS CAN BE BLEACHED of their resonance by overuse. The words "I love you" are either a great boost against despair or an empty platitude depending on the credibility of the speaker. But those of us who have known genuine love know its healing power for both the giver and the receiver. We know it to be at the very heart of the meaning of our lives.

Rabbi Moshe Leib of Sassov once told his disciples that he learned the meaning of love from two drunkards who were sitting in an inn drinking. They drank silently, but from time to time Ivan turned to Alexei and asked, "Do you love me?" "Yes, Ivan, I do. I am your friend." After they emptied another glass, Ivan asked again, "Alexei, Alexei, are you really my friend?" In anger Alexei replied, "How many times must I tell you, Ivan, that I am! You are my friend and my heart is full of love for you. Must I go on repeating it all night?" At that point Ivan looked at Alexei and shook his head sadly, "Alexei, Alexei, if you *are* my friend, then how come you don't know what is hurting me?"[1] We can be so preoccupied with our own needs that we fail to open ourselves to others and do not appreciate either their joy or their pain.

To love we must allow ourselves to be extended so that we can truly share the joy of another, feel the other's pain, and be moved to ease it. This is not as simple a matter as it appears. Consider the relation of husband and wife. When I am conducting weddings, I remind bride and groom of God's words before creating Adam, "It is not good for man to dwell alone; I will make him a helpmate." The two Hebrew words, *ezer-k'negdo*, usually translated as "a helpmate against him" or "his opposite" have a double-edged meaning. They can mean either someone who will stand supportively *beside* him or one who will stand against him ("an intimate enemy").

The marital bond confers unsurpassed power to hurt or heal. Each partner knows the buttons to push, the words or deeds that will increase the pain of the other. In virtually all human relationships there will be moments we feel impelled to hurt the other. Rare are the lovers who have never hurt their beloved by word or deed. No less significant is our power to heal our intimate other.

In one of my visits to the hospital, I observed one spouse lovingly attending her husband, diligently responding to and even anticipating his needs. Her mood reflected the current condition of her beloved. There were unguarded moments when her face registered an aching weariness tinged with exhaustion and self-pity. But such feelings were overwhelmed by her desire to be there to comfort her mate.

One woman who nursed her husband through a terminal illness remarked to me that she felt privileged to discover during those difficult months that she loved her husband even more than she had thought possible.

During such encounters I often imagine this couple at their wedding, young and strong, as they promised to be there for each other in sickness and in health. Life often calls us to redeem those promises. Most genuine love entails some measure of self-sacrifice.

Joan and I had just returned from visiting her mother in an ICU cubicle. There Fannie lay restlessly in her bed, sustained by a respirator after open heart surgery that was followed by additional surgery a week later to seal a perforated ulcer. The initial surgery was deemed urgent to bring sufficient oxygen into her lungs. In her eighties, Fannie was mentally agile. Fully aware of the risks of her surgery, she decided to proceed anyway.

Her postoperative condition was critical. She would be awake for a while, then lapse into a fitful slumber induced by weariness and medication. While we were there Fannie opened her eyes. We stood by her bed, knowing as she no doubt knew that these were her last days. We kissed her hand and told her we loved her. Unable to speak she put her hand to her lips and threw us a kiss. In that dimly lit ICU cubicle with all its artificial support systems and images projected on a screen, no monitor recorded the flow of love that bathed that gloomy space with its radiance. Those moments were sad and painful but also strangely beautiful.

Many times in our lives we discover that beauty and sadness are intertwined. Almost always love is the link between them. Love brings enormous pain to such moments. Paradoxically, love also washes such moments in the precious awareness of what makes life worth living.

Every year, during our summer vacations at the lake, we worship with a small congregation in Petoskey, Michigan. There are so few children that a bar or bat mitzvah is an event for the entire community. Stacy Holden's was the first bat mitzvah in the synagogue. Several years later this pretty, vivacious young woman was afflicted with a rare neurological disease that progressively immobilized her. Stacy strove valiantly to live a full and normal life. She married and bore two girls. As her illness progressed, her marriage collapsed. With the love and support of her parents, she continued to work as a lab technician and raised her daughters, Jamie and Erika.

One summer, Stacy introduced me to Tim and asked me to officiate at their marriage. The bride had to be carried to the *chuppah*, the bridal canopy, by her groom. She sat in a wheelchair during the ceremony. Tim embraced Stacy's faith and was an extraordinarily devoted and loving husband.

Stacy and Tim were married only a few years before her condition deteriorated. Remarkably, Stacy confounded the doctors by bounding back from death's door again and again. One Friday evening, Stacy was at services, propped up in a soft armchair with Tim at her side. She could no longer speak. At that Sabbath service, her daughter Jamie was to become Bat Mitzvah, a daughter of the covenant. Jamie conducted the service as her mother had done twenty-two years earlier. The little synagogue was overflowing with congregants, family, neighbors, and friends.

After Jamie read from the Torah, she spoke briefly. She thanked her grandparents and "especially my mom for teaching me so much of my Judaism." At that point Stacy responded to her daughter's tribute with a shrill groan. Jamie broke down and sobbed. There was not a dry eye among us. Jamie got through the service and so did her mother. Our little synagogue was drenched in a love that sustained Jamie and transformed her Bat Mitzvah into a sad but incredibly precious day. A few weeks later, Stacy died. Once again an outpouring of love from family, congregation, and the entire community of that little town helped nourish Tim and Stacy's daughters.

Despite its amazing power, love is no magic potion that conquers all. Someone who battles deep depression needs therapy before he or she will be able to care deeply about anything or anyone. But some may discover in the course of their struggle against despair that love is what empowers them to choose life.

Jane was a bright, strong-willed woman afflicted with recurring assaults of depression. I knew that her four children were grown and that some years before, she had left an unhappy marriage. She never actually joined my congregation but she attended services occasionally and told me she was "intrigued" by my sermons. Sporadically she made efforts to engage me in conversation and occasionally she kept in touch through correspondence.

Jane always impressed me as being a religious skeptic and a faith seeker at the same time. Her analytical mind marshaled formidable arguments against faith in God but there was a hunger in her soul. She doubted and wondered, resisted and sought. She once shared a poem with me written in the aftermath of an attack of depression: "Morning has dawned again / but night too will soon descend / One needs to know when one is beaten and bow out."

Days after writing that poem, Jane was able to say, "I don't want to kill myself, I don't want to die. This whole miracle has so much to offer." On another occasion, Jane wrote, "The meaning in my life I find in my relation with my children and grandchildren. . . . One granddaughter telephones me late one night with a serious problem and concludes our long conversations saying, 'There is no one else I could have talked to about this,' or another granddaughter writes, 'Knowing that you are with me in spirit helps to bolster my confidence and lessen my fears.' " Prozac, or some equivalent, may be today's miracle drug, but the elixir of love is God's oldest prescription against despair.

So far, we have focused on love within the family. But if our lives are truly graced, we also discover the balm of love beyond the family circle. I shall never forget a dinner at our home prior to our youngest daughter's wedding. The groom's dearest friend and best man rose to toast my daughter. He described himself as a "tough cop" and then broke into tears as he held the cup of wine and expressed his love for the groom.

If love of friends can enhance a joyful moment, how much the more cherished is that love when we are hurting. A teenager who experienced the terrifying trauma of rape recalled for me the vital role of a friend who listened, encouraged, and was just present for a hug and a good cry. "Rabbi," she confided, "I don't know how I could have gotten through those months without Matt."

On National Public Radio one morning, I heard a story of a young man who dropped out of high school. He had been in and out of jail since then and was struggling to make it straight. During the interview, he allowed himself a rare moment of warm sentiment when he confided to his buddy how much his friendship meant. "Hey, man, I couldn't make it without you." Startled, but deeply moved, his friend hugged him. Afterward, the young man told the journalist reporter, with his voice cracking, "That's the first time I was ever hugged by a man." He had never known his father.

Certain persons seem to have cultivated or been gifted with an extraordinary capacity to love those outside the circle of family or friendship. Our world tends to respond with suspicion and cynicism to the notion of saintly persons. We know our limited capacity for love and we have reason to suspect the motives of those who appear to be acting with undo selflessness. We stigmatize them as masochists or assume some hidden angle. But even as some people exhibit awesome virtuosity in art, music, or philosophy, there are others who exhibit an uncommon capacity for selfless love. Edith Wyschogrod, a philosopher of religion, defines a saint as "one whose adult life in its entirety is devoted to the alleviation of sorrow (the psychological suffering) and pain (the physical suffering) that afflicts other persons without distinction of rank or group . . . whatever the cost to the saint in pain or sorrow."[2] Most of us are more likely to respond with sacrificial love to those whose lives are intimately intertwined with our own. The saintly person is moved to offer a loving response not on the basis of proximity or kinship, but only by the depth of the other's need.

Although most of us do not claim the saintly track as our own, at times we too encounter a selfless love for the stranger in either ourselves or others. In much of our contemporary life, our neighbor may well be a stranger whom we glimpse fleetingly as we press the door opener and drive into our garage. Since most of us are not saints, the love we can feel for such a neighbor or a stranger is not the same as the love we feel toward a spouse or a child.

Still there are times when we instantly bond with other human beings or feel they have bonded with us. We experience their pain as our own and are overcome by the desire to be a caring presence for them if only for that time. I link this capacity for great empathy to the Bible's core affirmation that we are all created in the divine image. Not always or even frequently but at least occasionally we do see in the stranger the image of God.

Such love or empathy comes more easily when there is shared pain. In a hospital waiting room I have often been struck by the instant camaraderie of those who sit and wait. They talk to each other, easily sharing their family member's medical situation, and seek to ease each other's anguish. In months to come, they may never encounter each other again but during that time in the waiting room, class distinctions and racial or religious differences become irrelevant as a special bond of empathy is forged.

Even in the absence of shared anxiety or shared hope, from time to time we can see in a stranger the image of God and are moved by genuine love. On many occasions in my life I have been the giver or receiver of such love. The brief encounter may occur on a plane in flight when I have become the instant confidant of a fellow passenger who expects never to see me again, or when I have allowed myself to share whatever is on my mind.

To be sure, it may be easier to feel love for a stranger whom we shall never see again than to feel such sentiments for a person with whom we have an ongoing relationship such as a coworker or a relative. The tensions of envy and competitiveness may be inevitable, but even those relationships can be changed qualitatively when we allow ourselves to see the fragile humanity in others.

In pastoral visits to the hospital or in counseling sessions in my office I have also felt this kind of love. Not always, but sometimes, I feel I am more than the performer of a professional duty. I am aware of reaching out in love to one in whom I perceive the image of God.

Sincere love for a child of God, however, must be distinguished from the potentially violating seductiveness of a counselor or clergyperson who exploits the vulnerability of a counselee. The boundary between one and the other must be vigilantly observed. The counselor must guard against that self-deception that leads to manipulative violations under the supposed guise of love and healing. Such violation of boundaries is never permissible. It destroys the trust that is an intrinsic part of being a healing presence in someone else's life.

During my own days in the hospital following serious surgery, I experienced two kinds of caregiving. One of my nurses was determined to establish her authority and medical proficiency. She seemed more moved to assert her power over me than to express her empathy for me. Her manner was abrupt and cold. That demeanor changed drastically when she saw that the president of the hospital came to visit and when my room received a procession of nonattending physicians. Suddenly she addressed me with terms of endearment and unctuously expressed great concern for my comfort and welfare. The turnabout was amusing, but disturbing.

I felt a palpable difference in the attitude of my night nurse. She embodied a quiet competence, empathy, and respect. She knew nothing about the social standing or professional prestige of any patients on her floor, yet I am confident she showed the same comforting and healing qualities to each of them. The hallmark of such love is consideration and respect for all human beings irrespective of what they can do for us or what we will get in return.

Over many years, I have noted two responses to personal adversity and suffering. Some bruised by adversity respond with anger, bitterness, and a numbing, self-serving cynicism: *What's the use of caring? Life is so unfair. I'm not going to permit myself to get hurt.* Reeling from the disappointments of love, they vow to spare themselves the pain of any deep emotional attachment. Overwhelmed by bitter disappointments, they retreat into an emotional safety zone that blocks out any thought of ever seeking to repair the brokenness of God's world. In their experience of life's pain, they find a warrant for a defensive philosophy of self-preservation and the exploitative use of others.

We know that those who have experienced abuse in an earlier stage of life may well become abusers of others. There are also others who have suffered abuse and, because of it, are more sensitive to the pain of others. Those who have "known the heart of the stranger" should be moved to respond with compassion, tenderness, and a heightened sense of justice on their behalf.

Murph was a tall, sturdy, black masseur at our local health club. He grew up in poverty in rural Louisiana. I once asked him, "How did you learn to laugh so heartily? Your laughter can light up a room." He told me, "Rabbi, I guess I learned it as a way of getting along, it helped with the pain." Murphy's pain was not confined to childhood. At age twenty-three he was blinded in an accident while working as a mechanic. He was also partially disabled and was taught his current profession by another blind masseur.

When I asked him one day, "Murph, how's it going?" He replied, "Oh, pretty well, I'm making it, Rabbi." Pausing for a moment, he added reflectively, "I don't know what happened to the magic wand I read about as a kid; I guess one's got to learn to live without that wand." I responded, "Suppose you had that magic wand, Murph, what would you wish for?" "Oh, Rabbi, you're playing a game I can't let myself play." "Play it," I urged. "How would you use that wand? What would be first?"

"Oh, Rabbi," he said, "hunger's always bothered me a whole lot . . . that anyone should be hungry. I'd use it to wish away hunger." Overwhelmed by Murphy's response, I continued, "And wish number two?" "Oh, I guess I would wish all the politicians were honest," he said with a chuckle. "But Murph, you asked nothing for yourself, what about you?" Pausing a moment, Murph exclaimed, "Doggone it, Rabbi, sometimes I forget I'm blind. I'd wish my sight back."

Many times the Bible enjoins us, "You shall not oppress a stranger, for you know the feelings of the stranger, having yourselves been strangers in the land of Egypt." Although the "Egypts" in our lives may make us more or less sensitive to the strangers we encounter, the religious commandment is clear and unequivocal. We are to remember our pain by responding with greater empathy and love to those who have also experienced the bitterness of life.

Those who have given such love are often blessed by its power to bring healing to themselves. I like to think of the *shammas,* the serving candle of the Chanukah menorah that is used to light the other candles. Like this candle, we are not diminished by offering the light of love to another. Quite the contrary, reaching out to those who like ourselves know the tragic dimension of life may be a source for our own healing. Such was surely the case with Joan Dater, who suffered a catastrophic loss when her only daughter was killed in the Pan Am crash over Lockerbie, Scotland. Relatives of victims formed a support group. Seven years later, Joan was transfixed by the news on television of TWA Flight 800 exploding in midair. She immediately wanted to help the families of victims of this disaster.

As she later told a *New York Times* reporter, "[the members of the support group] do not know how they would have endured without the group they formed to support one another." Watching news of the TWA disaster made it seem as if her daughter Gretchen had died all over again. Upon hearing the news, Joan's support group reached out to the families of those lost in the TWA crash. They knew the pain of sudden loss and wanted to help. This act of love, born of their own grief, no doubt brought a measure of healing to the givers of love as well as its receivers.[3]

Martin Buber has pointed to the love of another as the highest form of spirituality. Buber taught that there are two modes of relating to the world, "I-It and I-Thou." An "I-It" orientation is emotionally detached, rational, objective, analytical—and goal-oriented. It connotes a utilitarian relationship in which things (or persons) are used as a means to an end, rather than an end in themselves.

The I-It mode is the appropriate relationship for certain situations. When a loved one enters the operating room, I want a surgeon who is in an "I-It" mode; he or she should be focused not on the person but on the affected organ or organs. I want the surgeon to apply medical knowledge and technical skills to perform a successful operation.

By contrast, an "I-Thou" relationship is not governed by a quest to produce a premeditated outcome. In such encounters two persons fully open themselves to each other. Each is fully present in mind, body, and spirit. "I-Thou" is the mode in which we discover our capacity to love and be loved unconditionally. This relationship is marked by empathy and caring for another who, like ourselves, is a child of God. Thus Buber defined love as the acceptance of responsibility of an "I" for a "Thou."

In my work at the Texas Medical Center I try to help medical students understand that to be an effective healer a physician must not only master the bio-science and apply it effectively to address the disease ("I-It"); the physician must also connect to the person in the patient and seek to understand how the disease is affecting that person's life ("I-Thou"). The surgeon in the operating room is understandably in an "I-It" mode, but when the surgeon meets with the patient before and after surgery, a healing encounter involves being fully present to the person and responding with caring and empathy. A caring doctor should be able to understand and respond to the fear, pain, and hopes of the patient.

During his struggle with prostate cancer, the literary critic Anatole Broyard wrote a series of articles about the experience of illness. His feeling about himself at that time had a lot to do with how doctors treated him. He wrote:

I wouldn't demand a lot of my doctor's time; I just wish he would *brood* on my situation for perhaps five minutes, that he would give me his whole mind just once. . . . Just as he orders blood tests and bone scans of my body, I'd like my doctor to scan *me*, to grope for my spirit as well as my prostate.[4]

In contrast, my friend Victoria claimed that her doctor's dedication encouraged her to keep fighting her disease. Victoria was diagnosed with metastatic breast cancer. For eight years, she battled the disease with multiple chemotherapies and experimental protocols as well, but all her remissions were very short-lived. Through it all, this strong and mature woman continued to be a mother to her two teenage children and maintain her executive position at an insurance company.

In one of our phone conversations, she asked me what I was doing in retirement. I told her of my efforts to help medical students understand that a healer must not only address the disease but connect with the patient, and that the quality of that connection can affect medical outcome. When I asked Victoria what enabled her to keep fighting her own disease, she answered without hesitation, "Wanting to be there for my children—and for my doctor." She explained that as a child she was taught that you shouldn't disappoint the people who really care for you. "My doctor not only gives me the best medical care, but I feel that he is on my side, fighting the battle with me. . . . I want to do well for him too."

A physician cannot be fully a healer if there is no "I-Thou" dimension in his or her practice. Buber maintained that we experience God through the caring presence of another, and that we, in turn, experience intimations of God's presence when we reach out in love to another human being. In my teaching, I suggest to future physicians that allowing themselves to care, paradoxically, will be their most powerful weapon against physician burnout.

We experience God's love most powerfully through the caring presence of others. And when the burdens of our own trouble and sorrow tempt us to grieve or despair, nothing is more restorative than to find in the face of another person the call for us to care, to nourish, and to love. In responding to that call, we often rediscover the significance and purpose of our own lives.

Our capacity to love is a divine gift. Because God has also endowed us with freedom, we have the power to love or to hate, to build or destroy. A couple bonded in the intimacy of marriage can be helpmates or "intimate enemies." In most human relationships, there are moments of each.

The biblical story of Adam and Eve identifies human sexuality with the loss of innocence. Unlike the animals in the forest, Adam eats of the Tree of Knowledge and therefore knows that he is naked. Sexuality is more than an instinctive drive for reproduction. For human beings, sex may be an expression of love or lust or even hate. Despite our culture's tendency to sentimentalize sex as a playful alternative to violence ("Make love, not war!") many of the four-letter words expressing hostility have patently sexual overtones. Sex is one of the many gifts we can use to fulfill or betray God's intention. Through sex we can love or hate, keep promises or violate them.

The rabbis understood this dual human capacity in terms of two conflicting impulses they call *yetzer ha-tov* (the good impulse) and *yetzer ha-ra* (the evil impulse). At times human life is an inner struggle between these impulses; at other times the sages declare that we need both impulses to fulfill God's intention for us. *Yetzer ha-ra*, the so-called evil impulse, is really the primal energy or passion without which we could do neither good nor evil. The *yetzer ha-tov*, the impulse for good, is our awareness of the direction for the proper deployment of that primal energy. When the two *yetzers* are united, passionate lovers are also respectful friends.

By virtue of these two urges, and our freedom to choose between them, we humans are the most noble and the most dangerous creatures on earth. So much pain and suffering in this world has been the result of the abuse of our primal energy. Has the time come when the human race cannot afford the freedom with which we have been endowed by our Creator? If we have the knowledge and power to wire ourselves for love, should we do so?

Such a scenario is depicted in Anthony Burgess's book, *A Clockwork Orange,* and the film based on it. This frightening work of science fiction tells the story of Alex, the leader of a teenage gang that has terrorized old and young with vicious acts of violence. Alex is caught, charged with second-degree murder, convicted, and imprisoned. While in prison, Alex agrees to participate in an elaborate experiment of conditioning through visual, auditory, and electrical stimuli. The experiment succeeds. Within two weeks, the vicious Alex is incapable of even fantasizing the violent acts of his past.

When the doctor in charge displays the "new" Alex, the prison chaplain diagnoses, "He ceases . . . to be a creature capable of moral choice." The doctor explains, "We are not concerned with motive, with higher ethics . . . only with cutting down crime." But as the book mentions earlier, "When a man cannot choose he ceases to be a man."[5]

The idea of an "engineered" human being is also explored in Stephen Spielberg's movie, *A.I.* (Artificial Intelligence), the story of a robotic child, David, who looks and acts almost like a human and is programmed to love. David is adopted by parents who have lost a young son. They hope the robotic David will in some way fill the void in their lives. David himself concludes the only way he will be considered worthy of his adopted family's love is if he becomes human.

Spielberg's movie dramatizes one of the critical boundaries that separate the robotic David from a human child. He is *programmed* to love. He does not have the freedom to choose between good and evil, between love and hate.

What makes goodness and love worthy of our admiration is that they are not a matter of conditioning or wiring but remain, to a significant degree, a human choice. Hence we are accountable for the way we choose to live. While it is tempting to reshape us or others into creatures incapable of imagining or devising evil, ours is a human adventure story precisely because we have been given great power and freedom. Human love is both a gift we choose to receive and a gift we can choose to bestow.

Before creating human creatures, say the rabbis, God consulted the angels. "Don't do it," they said. "Humans will be nothing but trouble." God ignored their advice. When God consulted a second group of angels, their response was the same and God ignored it. The third group replied, "What did it avail the former angels that spoke to you? The world is yours, do as you please!" Then God created Adam and Eve. As it turned out, the first generations were not very promising. Cain killed Abel, the generation of Noah was so wicked that God destroyed them in a flood, and the generation that followed built the Tower of Babel to laud their power and challenge God.

The surviving angels confronted God with the angelic equivalent of "We told you so. Now look what has happened." But God responded, "Nevertheless, I will forever put up with man."[6] God has faith that human beings may use their God-given gifts for a blessing. If God believes in us, can we have less faith in ourselves?

Chapter 9

Living in a Broken World

A twisted thing . . . cannot be made straight.
—Ecclesiastes 1:15

A PHOTOGRAPHER INVITES YOU to pose. She tries to capture your best angle and minimize the bald spot and the overly prominent nose. When the proofs are available she explains reassuringly, "Don't worry, I can touch it up, put some color in your cheeks, remove the lines on the forehead and the blemishes on the skin."

The photographer has a vision of physical wholeness, of what an ideal face looks like, and she does her best to recreate us in that image. We find a similar concern with "the right look" in a modeling agency or the office of the TV producer picking an anchorwoman. Even a pulpit selection committee will favor the rabbi or minister who has the right look. We value physical wholeness in others and in ourselves.

The Hebrew Bible also projects an image of physical wholeness. In Leviticus, God instructs Aaron the high priest on which of his descendants may preside at the altar. "No man of your offspring . . . who has a defect shall be qualified. . . . No man who is blind, or lame, or who has a limb too short or too long; no man who has a broken leg or a broken arm, or who is a hunchback, or a dwarf, or who has a growth on his eye, or has a boil-scar, or scurvy, or crushed testes . . . shall be qualified" (21:17-21).

This particular biblical text reflects more the ancient Israelite's view of perfection than God's. We, too, have our concept of physical wholeness. We also have greater resources than our ancestors to make whole what is physically broken. The woman who undergoes a mastectomy may request reconstructive surgery to restore her breasts. Ours is also the age of hip replacements, skin grafts, and organ transplants.

The Hebrew word for wholeness is *shalem*. Wholeness suggests completeness. Before Eve was created God said, "It is not good for man to be alone; I will make a fitting helper for him" (Genesis 2:18). In the Jewish mystical tradition, man and woman become complete by their marriage to each other. Parenthood is also a sign of wholeness. Our sages teach that when Jacob was surrounded by his children he felt *shalem b'vanav,* complete or "whole" by virtue of "his children."[1]

Completing tasks to which we have dedicated our lives or achieving primary goals may also foster a sense of wholeness. When King Solomon built the great Temple in Jerusalem, the artists and craftsmen and all the workmen felt this was the crowning work of their lives. Miraculously, we are taught, none of the workmen died until the Temple was finished. At that moment, *shalma nafsham*—"their lives were complete."[2]

I received a call from a retired colleague who during many years of an active rabbinate had struggled to finish a book about a famous medieval Jewish preacher. Year after year, I would hear he was still working on it. Now in retirement he called me from California to say, "I finished it. It's at the publisher and it's good." His voice cracked with the feeling of one who knew he had fulfilled a cherished goal.

A woman I know who dreamed of making another pilgrimage to Israel before she died, and another woman who wanted to live to attend her grandchild's wedding, each felt a deep completeness when the goal was attained. We all harbor a secret dream of what would make our lives complete and fulfilled.

Our images of aesthetic wholeness or perfection change over time. The artist Rubens regarded the plump, full-bodied women he painted as the quintessence of feminine perfection. In our culture those chosen to model high-fashion designs must be much thinner. To attain this ideal, women may subject themselves to rigorous diets, not always with great success. For some, that ideal slenderness is unattainable.

We nourish images of bodily health and wholeness that disease and accident may undermine. At age eleven, before the Salk vaccine, writer Leonard Kriegel contracted polio and became crippled for life. During his two years at the New York State Reconstruction Home he was not prepared to accept his fate.

> Like every other boy in the ward, I organized my needs around whatever illusions were available. And the illusion I needed above any others was that one morning I would simply wake up and rediscover the "normal" boy of memory, once again playing baseball in French Charley's Field in Bronx Park. . . . At the age of eleven I needed to weather reality, not face it. [3]

In this age of high-tech medicine, we pride ourselves on all the ways we can correct what is broken. But today most physicians will still spend a significant part of their days trying to palliate conditions for which there is presently no available cure. The promise of stem cell research has generated much excitement and hope, but many hurdles must be overcome before the fruit of this research will result in dramatic cures. The fact is that many persons now suffering with chronic conditions will live with those conditions rather than expect a cure in their lifetime. And, unless our new age is completely different from human life before us, we are all destined to experience some physical brokenness that is simply the price of our being human.

Even if we regard our degree of physical wholeness in this life as exemplary, there may be other forms of irreparable brokenness that assault us. Linda and Jack felt this brokenness after their son Nicholas died. Do parents ever fully heal from such a loss? Those spared the loss of a child or crippling disease will encounter other brokenness. No one lives and leaves this earth fully whole.

There is also that brokenness we call regret. An aspiring writer must acknowledge she will never write the great American novel. We dream of careers that circumstances render beyond our reach. My friend Milton envisioned becoming a physician. When the Great Depression wiped out his family's fortune, Milton was compelled to give up that dream. He worked all day and attended school at night. Later, when the woman he fell in love with could not adjust to New York City, he settled in her small southern town and became a merchant in his father-in-law's store. Milton always recalled wistfully the dream of a professional career that was never realized.

Some months before his death, the influential American philosopher and intellectual Sidney Hook agreed to be interviewed by *Commentary Magazine*. When asked about his regrets, Hook lamented that he had not received a better Jewish education or provided one for his children. He spoke of four grandchildren with much delight but then explained, "They have no Jewish consciousness." When the interviewer inquired, "And you regret this?" Hook responded, "Very much."[4]

At some point in life we may discover serious disappointments in our most significant relationships. Sadly, a friend confided to me that his father had been just a shadow in his life, vaguely present but not effectively supportive or influential in shaping his son's values. When his father died, he did not mourn, but just felt sad. He mourned the father he wished he had.

When a spouse has been betrayed by the infidelities of a mate, or when a person becomes fully conscious that he or she was abused by a parent, or a man feels cheated in a business relationship with his brothers—such a loss of trust may never be fully repaired. Our relationship to those persons may never be whole.

Hebrew Scripture itself suggests that we must come to terms with broken relationships that cannot be repaired. When the estranged brothers Jacob and Esau are reconciled after their dramatic reunion, they still choose not to live near one another. Instead they go their separate ways. This less than ideal conclusion is both sad and comforting. The Bible teaches us that the cumulative hurts of the past cannot always be erased and forgotten, even if they have been forgiven. Jacob and Esau reaffirm the fraternal bond but they are not able to live together. They come together only for such milestone events as the death and burial of their father Jacob (in Genesis 35:29) and even God does not demand more of them.

Unbidden and unwelcomed, irreparable brokenness intrudes upon all our lives. How may we cope with it? We must first take time to grieve. The Reverend Jerry Sittser lost his wife and two children in a tragic auto accident. He writes of "giving myself to grief. . . . Mostly I sat in my rocking chair and stared into space, reliving the accident and remembering the people I lost. I felt anguish in my soul and cried bitter tears."[5] Earlier we noted that Judaism provides a structure for grieving that includes staying at home for as much as a week to receive the comfort of friends, to recite Kaddish, the Mourner's Prayer, in the fellowship of at least ten other worshipers for a period of close to a year, and only gradually to return fully to life's normal patterns. Healing begins with grieving.

A time to grieve may also be required after a divorce or a total estrangement from a sibling or a parent or an adult child. We also grieve the shattering of bodily wholeness through disease or accident. All significant loss and disappointment demands time to nurse wounds and experience sadness and even anger.

My wife and I grieved after that fire destroyed our home. We do mourn the loss of material things: familiar chairs, family albums, well-marked books, the costumes belonging to my wife's dance company, and the place we called home for twenty years. In her note of condolence a friend sensitively observed, "We nest, and the twigs we accumulate and create and then carefully place as we build give us comfort, a sense of place and safety. To have your nest destroyed so suddenly must be overwhelming." It was.

In our case, however, the grieving over loss came later. In the midst of the fire all such grief was preempted by an experience that compelled us to reclarify our priorities. After the tremendous clap of thunder that started the fire, the lights dimmed and the phone went dead. My wife saw smoke and saw sparks dart from the dishwasher. I ran next door to call 911. When I returned to the house to see if Joan was still there and called out her name, there was no answer. Terrified, I ran upstairs, groped in the darkness and was almost overcome by the dense smoke. I ran downstairs and outdoors and desperately screamed, "Joan!" When my wife replied from a neighbor's house across the street, I was so grateful that I watched our home crumble before my eyes with relative composure.

There is no quick fix when we are confronted by the pain of an irreparable loss, but as we have seen, we can discover precious resources to cope with grievous hurts. The balm of religious faith is certainly central to my own quest for comfort. Sharing the burden in prayer with the Source of our being may help us discern that God is with us. Prayer may empower us to carry on with our lives, and in time lead to the healing of the spirit.

This faith is not an easy or steady possession. Even clergy may be assaulted by anguished doubt. The Reverend Jerry Sittser writes in the aftermath of his tragic loss:

> Pain seems to conceal [God] from us, making it hard for us to believe that there could be a God in the midst of our suffering. In our pain we are tempted to reject God, yet for some reason we hesitate to take that course of action. So we ponder and pray. We move toward God, then away from [God]. We wrestle in our souls to believe. Finally we choose God, and in this choosing we learn that [God] has already chosen us and has already been drawing us to [God].[6]

In the midst of our brokenness, many of us discern the "face of God" in those others who embrace us with their love and support. A woman who underwent a mastectomy told me of the immense comfort she derived from the counsel of another woman who had been through this loss before her. The Reverend Sittser was overwhelmed by those who entered his life to help him care for his three surviving children. A small group of men from the college where he teaches began meeting with him weekly after the accident to give support. He spoke of them as "a community of brokenness."

For many years I have cherished an old parable from an eighteenth-century Jewish preacher about a king who prized a huge perfect diamond. One night he was tormented by a dream that his flawless diamond was deeply scratched. He ordered his viceroy to bring the diamond from the vault and indeed, it was scratched!

That morning the king offered a great reward to anyone who could restore the diamond to its pristine perfection. Many came to the palace and tried to remove the scratch. One fixer recited incantations over the diamond, to no avail. Another dipped the gem in a magic solution; the scratch remained. Then an old man appeared with a sharp instrument. On the scratched surface he proceeded to engrave a beautiful rose and he used the scratch to make the stem.[7]

Not even God may remove all the scratches of our lives but God helps us use those scratches for a blessing. Many literary and visual artists have used the scratches in their lives to create the works of power and beauty that move us. Leonard Kriegel, his body broken by the scourge of polio, discovered through that disability his distinctive and powerful literary voice. Of his career as a writer Kriegel observes:

> With each word I wrote, I was searching for the boy who existed until I was eleven, when, as I melodramatically phrased it in my first book, *The Long Walk Home*, "the knife of virus severed legs from will, and I found myself flat on my back, paralyzed with polio." But that virus gave me a writer's voice.[8]

Frieda had gone on vacation with friends after graduating from college. During a break from sightseeing, she playfully climbed a tree. Her friends were amused until they watched her slip and fall. As a result of that accident, she became a paraplegic. Over many months she grieved and fought both rage and despair. In time, she was able to transmute her pain into a passionate mission to remove barriers in the environment that left her and others from being integrated into the full stream of life.

This mission lifted and energized Frieda's spirit. It gave new meaning to her life. As a political activist, she has lived to see the landmark Disabilities Act enacted into law. She has taught me that admiration for her human spirit must not distract me from the responsibility to help create a barrier-free environment for all who share her condition—and to do so not out of compassion, but as an act of justice. Frieda has made a good life for herself.

At some point we find healing of the spirit or inner wholeness in the midst of irreparable brokenness if we can begin to accept and love ourselves unconditionally. We must regain the power to see the image of God within us, to reclaim that inalienable dignity that is our birthright. We must also regain the power to see our loss as an integral part of our life and be able to say of the whole, "Behold, it is very good." My friend Milton, whose dream of becoming a physician was shattered by the Great Depression, did not permit that disappointment to embitter his days. He found satisfaction as a small-town merchant where he was known and respected by virtually everyone. He became a fanatical fan of a local college football team and made his wife and two sons the joyful center of his life.

Professor Sidney Hook, who deeply regretted that his grandchildren were bereft of any Jewish consciousness, pondered the question, "If you had a chance to relive your life, . . . would you accept that chance?" Dr. Hook answered, "I would."[9] Without denying the disappointment and pain, Sidney Hook would still gratefully accept his life in its entirety and call it good.

For the Reverend Sittser acceptance meant discovering that in time, the tragic accident could be placed in the context of his entire life as "a very bad chapter in a very good story."[10]

When the brokenness of life intrudes upon us, it shatters our sense of well-being and leaves us reeling in pain. We feel as if darkness at noon has enveloped us; we become broken shards strewn randomly on the ground. This much is certain: we will be transformed by the experience. *How* depends significantly on the way we respond to our brokenness.

In the best-case scenario, we can be deepened and ennobled by our encounters with irreparable loss. Many—not all—emerge from their time of trial with a greater closeness to God, a heightened appreciation of the daily miracles we have so easily taken for granted, a deeper compassion, and a desire to live and be a blessing to those who are touched by their lives. They have reclaimed meaning and have found a healing of the spirit, an inner wholeness in the midst of brokenness.

One form of brokenness lacks the high drama of estrangement from a loved one, a tragic accident, a crippling disease, or a natural disaster. Yet it is even more universal and inclusive in its embrace. All the great religious traditions highlight its impact on human life.

Some call it sin. Others speak of a brokenness of the spirit. The single time of the year that draws most Jews to the synagogue is the High Holy Day season. Rosh Hashanah (the Jewish New Year), and Yom Kippur (the Day of Atonement) usher in a time of critical self-examination and confession of failure. The liturgy offers a long, detailed litany of our spiritual brokenness prefaced by the words, "For these sins, O God of mercy, forgive us, pardon us, grant us atonement."[11]

Those of us who follow the religious script of this liturgy and engage in the public ritual of shared brokenness have not generally committed heinous crimes; we are not terrible people either in our eyes or in the eyes of others. In the balance, we might even claim to live reasonably decent lives. Yet if we open ourselves to honest self-scrutiny, we know we are not all that God—or we ourselves—would want us to be. As a close friend puts it, "There are holes in all our buckets."

We are not as considerate of others as we know we might be. We may permit an obsession with our work to eclipse our commitment to sharing more of the lives of our families. In moments of denial, we may plead economic necessity (I'm doing this for my family), but honesty compels us to admit that a relentless preoccupation with the job is also a way of avoiding demands of intimacy and responsibility at home.

In a moment of self-revelation, we may admit ego-centeredness that impairs our capacity to love more deeply and to care enough about those around us, including those to whom we are bound by kinship or friendship. At certain moments we could all echo the words from writer Alfred Kazin's journal, "It is suffocating to be so bound up in oneself. . . . I pray to get beyond myself. . . . I pray to be relieved of so much 'self,' I ask to be extended."[12]

The primary story of the High Holy Day season is that with God's help we can elevate the moral quality of our lives. Spiritual growth—repentance or return to the path God intends for us—is not only desirable but possible. We all know of lives, including our own, that have been dramatically turned around. Yet, as we make our inventory of the soul, we may also be overwhelmed by sadness. Despite all our resolutions to act differently, we realize each year that spiritual progress is uneven and a gap remains between the way we live and the way we feel we should live.

With high resolve, we vow each year to be different. We vow to be more spiritually mature, to be less slavishly dependent upon peer approval, to be freer of jealousy and envy, to truly delight in the attainments of another without deprecating ourselves. Each of us has an idealized image of how we would like to be and a personal list of the warts that stubbornly mar our spiritual profile. We are broken vessels aspiring to an ethical wholeness that eludes us. Sooner or later, we discover that the absence of wholeness is part of the human condition.

There is some comfort in knowing we are not alone. Shortly before his death, the Pulitzer Prize–winning novelist Bernard Malamud was working on another book. His younger colleague, Philip Roth, came to visit. Malamud showed him the beginning of the new manuscript. Roth read the opening chapters and felt the piece needed a lot more work. As discreetly as possible, Philip Roth asked, "What comes next?"

In a soft voice suppressing fury, Malamud said, "What's next is not the point." Malamud, acclaimed in his lifetime as one of America's premier writers of fiction, was visibly angry. Roth, who knew him well, explained, "[Malamud] was perhaps as angry at failing to master the need for assurance so nakedly displayed as he was with me for having nothing good to say. He wanted to be told that what he had painfully composed . . . was something more than he himself must have known it to be."[13] Malamud was more dependent than he liked on validation by others. The assured inner-directedness that is the mark of maturity had eluded him.

One of my friends, an accomplished psychoanalyst, has helped many people toward greater maturity and has of course been through a complete analysis himself. He once confided to me his lingering crises of confidence when he doubts the adequacy of his powers or the efficacy of his labors. My friend reminded me that such moments of anguished self-doubt and self-denigration go with the human territory, even with self-awareness, even after psychoanalysis, even if you are an analyst.

I take the High Holy Day message of judgment and spiritual renewal very seriously, but after many years I am more aware than ever how far I am from my vision of perfect maturity or spiritual wholeness. At such times I find comfort in the biblical and rabbinic portrait of Moses, arguably the greatest figure in the Hebrew Bible. Moses shared his leadership role with seventy elders. Two of the elders, Eldad and Medad, did not wait for Moses to consecrate them. They began prophesying on their own. When Joshua, Moses' loyal aide, reported the matter to his chief, Moses responded graciously, "Are you [jealous] on my account? Would that all the LORD's people were prophets, that the LORD put his spirit upon them!" (Numbers 11:29). How selflessly magnanimous!

The stories of the rabbinic sages often amplify and sometimes challenge the adequacy of a biblical portrait, by fleshing out the details. In the Bible, God tells Moses that he will get a glimpse of the promised land but will not live long enough to enter it. According to one rabbinic *Aggadah,* Moses appealed the verdict. He implored God, "Lord, let me live a little longer. I don't mind Joshua being in control. I'm not jealous of my successor. I know I'm retired but let me just go over to the promised land and observe from the sidelines."

So God tested Moses and let him follow Joshua around for a day. At one point Joshua, the new leader of the people, entered the Tent of Meeting to commune alone with God. Instinctively Moses moved toward the entrance of the tent and when he realized he could no longer enter, he felt deeply jealous of Joshua. Moses turned to God and said, "There are times when death is sweeter than life. I'm ready God, take me."[14]

For all his religious faith and closeness to God not even Moses was fully liberated from the human condition. Not even he fully transcended the spiritual brokenness of human life.

Beyond the consolation of sharing spiritual brokenness with some pretty impressive people, the perspective of faith offers another healing gift. About twenty-four hundred years ago, Ezra, the scribe, and Nehemiah, the Jewish governor of Judea, assembled a small congregation of Israelites in an outdoor sanctuary. This convocation took place on the first day of the Hebrew month of *Tishri* (Nehemiah 8). It was Rosh Hashanah. The people offered prayers of praise to God. Ezra opened the Torah scroll that contains God's commandments. He read that in the wilderness the Israelites had often failed to abide by those commandments.

When the people measured their own lives against the teachings of the Torah, they broke down and wept. They felt so worthless. Then Nehemiah made this remarkable statement, "Don't weep. This day is holy to the Lord. Dress up and eat and send portions to those who are in need [so they can eat too] because the delight of the Lord is your strength" (Nehemiah 8:10, paraphrased).

On the Day of Judgment (Yom Kippur), Nehemiah preached to the people: Don't torture yourselves because you haven't perfectly fulfilled the covenant. Let God's delight—God's acceptance of you in your humanness—be your strength. By all means strive to grow and move toward spiritual wholeness. You can make significant changes for the better, but keep perspective. God respects the rough edges of your life. God does not expect you to play a perfect game; neither should you. God accepts you in your brokenness; therefore, you can accept yourself. God's delight in your humanness is your strength.

The capacity to accept ourselves and others in our spiritual brokenness is grounded in the deep faith that the God of justice is also a God of unconditional love and forgiveness. If God accepts us in our brokenness, shall we be less generous to ourselves than the Source of our being? And shall we be less generous to others?

There is often a correlation between our attitude toward others and ourselves. At a certain stage in life, we may overidealize our parents. Later we may judge them too harshly for those flaws we most detest in ourselves. As we move toward what psychiatrist Erik Erikson calls integrity or wholeness, it is easier to accept our parents as they are and to forgive them. We are able to love them in their brokenness if we have learned to love and accept ourselves. Such acceptance is an important part of coping with life's darker side. It is part of the healing of our spirit.

When I returned from a speaking engagement in another city, I received a letter from a stranger who had been in attendance. Anne described herself as "not a happy person." She was deeply troubled by the people in her world. So many people she once admired had disappointed her. She asked, "What's happened to truth and integrity, Rabbi?' Anne's older brother had admonished her to be more accepting of people's inadequacies. "I can't do that," she wrote me, "without losing my own integrity."

Anne was an angry woman. Rereading her letter brought to mind a famous and often angry rabbi, Menachem Mendl of Kotzk. The rabbi's disciples once asked him to explain a verse in Genesis in which Rachel complained bitterly to Jacob, her husband, on account of her barrenness and the text says, "Jacob was enraged." The Rabbi of Kotzk's disciples asked him, "Why was Jacob enraged? None of the other patriarchs exhibited a similar anger with their barren wives." Even though Jacob was certain he was not a factor in her barrenness (this was a prescientific age), why didn't Jacob's compassion for Rachel restrain him from answering her so harshly?

In his response the Rabbi of Kotzk cited a verse from the prophet Micah that says that God "gave truth to Jacob." He explained, "He who sees the world (only) with the attribute of truth is likely to be angry." Those in whom the passion for truth and perfection is untempered by compassion for human brokenness are likely to be angry much of the time. Perhaps the Rabbi of Kotzk was thinking of his own bitterness.[15]

The single-minded commitment to truth may lead us to be offended by all imperfection in ourselves or others. This mind-set may suit a prophet but it ill suits Jacob, the patriarch, or the Rabbi of Kotzk, or any of us who wishes to live with others in this world. An *Aggadah* about the second-century sage, Rabbi Simeon ben Yohai, illustrates the perils of rigid perfectionism that spawns disdain for all who reject our way. Simeon and his son Eleazer lived during the time of Roman persecution in the land of Israel. For denigrating the Romans, Simeon and his son needed to go into hiding in a cave. They spent their days in study and prayer. After twelve years had passed, the prophet Elijah informed them that Caesar was dead and his decrees annulled. At that point, Simeon and his son emerged from the caves. When they saw people "plowing and sowing [rather than studying Torah], Rabbi Simeon exclaimed, 'These men forsake life eternal and engage in temporal life!' Whatever they cast their eyes upon was immediately incinerated. At that, a divine voice went forth and said, 'Have you come out to destroy My world? Return to your cave!' "[16]

I wrote to Anne, "Your moral indignation and passion for truth and justice is to be highly valued; however, even the prophets struggled with the tension between justice and love. They recognized that none of us could pass muster if God were only to relate to us as true judge and not also as loving parent. We need to be accountable for our words and actions, but we and others also need understanding and acceptance in the midst of brokenness. It has become easier for me to forgive my parents their flaws as I have become better at forgiving my own."

If the passion for truth and commitment to perfection make us persistently angry or depressed, we will be very unhappy. Wholeness and healing require an acceptance of ourselves and others in our nobility and our brokenness.

In the biblical vision, perfect wholeness, harmony, and order will elude us until the Messianic Age. We cannot create or expect it in ourselves or the world. In his novel *Local Anaesthetic,* Günter Grass writes of a dentist who claims he has found a perfect preventive for tooth decay. The novel ends with the patient's reference to a new problem, "As for me, an abscess has formed on the lower left. . . . The abscess was scraped out. . . . Nothing lasts. There will always be pain."[17] The message is clear: In this world we had better seek local anesthetics and provisional answers rather than expect perfect solutions to life's most recalcitrant problems.

By human effort alone, we cannot bring to pass the Messianic Age, when "the wolf shall dwell with the lamb" (Isaiah 11:6) and escape unharmed, any more than we can make a world where "every man shall sit under his grapevine or fig tree / With no one to disturb him" (Micah 4:4)—or a world where there is no pain, decay, or loss.

God alone can bring the ultimate fulfillment of the divine dream. Our human task is to help repair what we can in that corner of God's world entrusted to our care: we must work for justice, healing, peace, and reconciliation even as we live with a brokenness we cannot fully mend, and envision a perfection we cannot fully achieve. After we have done our best, we must place our faith in the redeeming power and love of our Creator.

Chapter 10

Sustaining Faith in Our Later Years

Your old . . . shall dream dreams, / And your young . . .
shall see visions. —Joel 3:1

A FEW SUMMERS AGO, Israel Charny, one of my dearest childhood friends, traveled from his home in Jerusalem to the Texas Medical Center for the removal of a cancerous bladder. The surgery went well and after a month-long convalescence my friend was ready to return home. Before leaving he turned to me and said, "You and I are on the last leg of our life journey. May it be a good one."

He knew that we were both approaching the end of our sixth decade. We had each recently undergone serious surgery. We had each been blessed with a productive and fulfilling life, and we were both willing and eager to do lots more significant living if empowered to do so.

We were also each contemplating retirement. He had given up his office in Tel Aviv and his chairmanship of the Program for Advanced Studies in Integrative Psychotherapy at Hebrew University. I was preparing to become Rabbi Emeritus at the congregation I had served for twenty-four years. The prospect of retirement, which was both enticing and frightening, provided the grist for a spirited conversation about our hopes for the future.

We had already shared the quip attributed to Bette Davis that "old age is no place for sissies," and repeated the cliché, "It sure beats the alternative." We knew this next stage of life would threaten us with brokenness of body, if not spirit, and we dared hope for years of usefulness, love, continued learning, and an even more intense savoring of life's simple pleasures.

We each knew that contemplating the next stage raised sobering questions. Would we continue to feel fulfilled as persons once we traded the satisfactions and stresses of our present life for the greater leisure of retirement? I had asked myself these questions many times. Would I find it difficult relinquishing a leadership role in a congregation I had served for so many years? Would I feel a painful sense of loss not preaching regularly or presiding at life-cycle ceremonies? Could I sit in a pew after forty years of leading a congregation in worship? What would it feel like to be marginalized, confined to the sidelines of life? What could I learn from those who have already dealt with these issues? What wisdom does my faith offer me for such a time?

Martin Marty is an ordained Lutheran minister who for thirty years has been a distinguished scholar and teacher of the history of religious movements in America. He is an incredibly prolific writer, a widely sought lecturer, and arguably the most interviewed expert in America on current religious trends.

I first got to know Marty when I served a congregation in Chicago and taught at the University of Chicago Divinity School. I both admired and coveted his amazing discipline and productivity. But what impressed me most was that he also managed to be a nurturing mentor to students, a devoted husband and father, and, for all his celebrity status, a sensitive human being. When he was with you, he would always take an interest in your life and work rather than impress you with his latest award or achievement.

More than a year before my retirement I learned that Marty at age seventy was retiring from a teaching position at the university and had given up other significant leadership roles. In a reflective article written for the *Park Ridge Center Bulletin,* he pondered the next stage of his life. He promised to take more long walks and exercise, to nurture old and new friendships, to deepen the already strong bond to his religious community, and to devote more time to the cause of justice in the inner city. He would now be free of some structured demands on his time and energy but hoped to continue to write, speak, and be a constructive presence in God's world. He wrote, "*Vocation* remains, career pattern changes. . . . Life is . . . a call to responsibility to others. . . . Each of us is irreplaceable, and we have to take pains to find out what the call means after retirement or job change."[1]

Those words resonated with me as I considered my own retirement from my congregation. I, too, hoped to enjoy relief from many of the burdens of my previous life. As one reaches my age, the multiple demands of congregational work become overly wearying. I promised to make more time for family and friends, baseball and tennis. I would enjoy reading the morning papers more leisurely, attending more games, spending more quiet evenings at home, and enjoying Sabbaths devoid of the pressure of preaching and conducting the service. I recall a rabbinic colleague who, when asked why he left the rabbinate to become a stockbroker, quipped, "So I could really observe the Sabbath."

At this writing, I can say I have done and enjoyed almost all of the things I promised to make time for. A few weeks after my official retirement I clipped an article from a magazine for my preaching files. Suddenly I thought, "Why am I doing this? I am retired." But the voice within me answered crisply, "Keep clipping, you'll find ways of using that article.

After all, you are retiring from the position of Senior Rabbi—not from the world."

In religious terms, our covenant with God does not end with retirement. At every stage of the life cycle God calls, "Where are you? What have you done this day to sanctify and enhance my world?" At every stage of life there are deeds we can perform as God's active servants in this world. This is our covenantal responsibility. If we are truly attentive, we will continue to hear the call summoning us to new tasks throughout our lives, even after retirement.

Those of us who have retired from satisfying and meaningful positions may feel we have earned the right to complete self-indulgence and should fill our days with golf, fishing, travel, browsing on the Internet, watching our investments, and consuming a variety of entertainments. But such self-absorption can be hazardous to our health. To be human is to need a significant purpose to our life. Complete self-indulgence may leave that need unfulfilled.

There is an integral relationship between the health of our body and the well-being of our spirit. We nourish our spirit when we permit ourselves to enjoy life's pleasures, but we human creatures need to be needed. We must feel we can still make a difference and be a blessing in God's world.

I know of people retired from long careers who have found new ways to harness their experiences and to engage their energies. Some remain part-time consultants in business, others mentor persons who want to sponsor new businesses and bring more jobs to inner-city neighborhoods. In my own city, the United Way draws special strength from retired executives who serve this vital charitable organization. At a recent conference I met a retired physician who lives in a small New England town. With deep satisfaction he told me he spends a few days a week at a medical clinic that serves the working poor who cannot afford health insurance. Such retired persons are less likely to suffer the malaise of uselessness. They are more likely to find meaning in their later years.

I now have completed my second year as a retired rabbi. Happily I can report that the added freedom to "smell the roses" and the greater leisure have been good because I have also continued to tend the garden in that little corner of the world entrusted to my care. I have preached, taught, and counseled. I have become a part-time Visiting Professor of Health and the Human Spirit at the University of Texas Health Science Center, and I am writing this book. My childhood friend continues to make significant contributions through his writing, lecturing, and counseling. When one door closes another opens, if we are attentive.

Over the years I have encountered many people who are inspiring models for the last stage of the life journey. Although Harriet Grossfield and Pearl Rowe live in quite different worlds, they share the blessing of a good old age.

Harriet recently celebrated her eighty-fifth birthday. For many years Harriet was an active partner in her husband Avery's career as a rabbi. Her warmth, spirituality, and exuberant disposition, as well as her literary skills and critical judgment, served Avery and the members of their congregation well. When Harriet was widowed thirty years ago, she worked as a secretary to support her family. Ten years ago she accepted a room in the Jewish nursing home in exchange for a commitment to be an unofficial staff person specializing in the comfort and nurture of the home's residents. The arrangement has worked well. Harriet has not only edited the newspaper for the home, but was also elected and reelected as president of the Residents' Council. She has championed the residents' welfare and acted as ombudsman to the administration in their behalf. Harriet also made sure that the local clergy knew if one of their members was particularly in need of attention.

During these years she has undergone a number of surgeries for cancer and has suffered from other vagaries of aging. Generally, her spirit has remained high, her sense of humor and capacity for laughter undimmed. At an annual meeting of the nursing home, which drew many community leaders as well as residents and their families, Harriet was invited to be one of the speakers. That day she told the assemblage:

> Last December, I celebrated my eighty-fifth birthday. In spite of two years of illness and three major surgeries, I refused to let all of this get me down. I stay cheerful because I believe in the incredible power of the human mind and spirit enabling me to fill my heart with faith and hope. . . . My faith in God's goodness has sustained me in every crisis of my life. Let me close with three quotes from the book of Psalms, they were the last words I whispered before my surgeries, "This is the day which the Lord has made, rejoice and be glad in it"; "God is our refuge and our strength"; "Be strong and let your heart take courage."

After that heady speaking engagement, Harriet suffered a three-week siege of pneumonia complicated by an adverse reaction to the codeine administered to suppress her rib-straining coughing spells. This illness left her physically exhausted and depressed. For days she turned off her phone and refused to see or speak even with old friends. Later, fully cognizant of what she had endured, Harriet demonstrated once again the resilience of her spirit. In our last phone conversation she was exuberant and even exhibited her trademark concern for the well-being of those around her. Once again she was championing the welfare of her residents.

As of this writing, Pearl Rowe has celebrated her ninety-fourth birthday. My wife and I have known Pearl for more than thirty years, ever since we started spending summers in Charlevoix, Michigan. When her husband Johnny was alive, he and Pearl decided to spend their retirement years in a little home on Lake Michigan. On their ample back acreage they planted vegetables and flowers. For years one of the high points of our summers was a visit to "Rowe's Garden" to pick carrots, raspberries, and tomatoes, and to select bouquets of fresh-cut flowers for our Sabbath table.

Johnny has been gone for about ten years now and Pearl no longer raises vegetables. Her hearing is impaired and macular degeneration has severely dimmed her vision, yet she continues to plant and tend her flowers. In a sprightly color-coordinated work outfit, Pearl labors for hours in the garden. Much as she enjoys just looking at the beauty she and God have wrought, Pearl also loves to pick her flowers, caress them lovingly, and arrange bouquets for area churches and the many visitors to the garden.

When Pearl works in the garden she loses track of time, forgets her aches and pains, and feels she is fulfilling a sacred vocation by cultivating and sharing with others the loveliness of God's creation. Apart from her children, grandchildren, and the precious memories of a life shared with Johnny, she finds healing of spirit by working six days a week in her garden.

Pearl confessed that during the last Christmas season she had managed to consume eleven pounds of chocolate candy. She vowed to watch her weight and her cholesterol. "After all, I'm ninety-four going for one hundred and the folks in town are rooting for me." Pearl has a thirty-six-year-old grandson who accepted a position in Mancelona, Michigan, thirty miles from Pearl's home in Charlevoix. When her grandson suggested that he buy a home near her she asked him if he had checked out the driving between Charlevoix and Mancelona in the winter months. She assured him that much as she would love to have him closer, she didn't want him to travel those roads if he could find a home near the plant where he worked. Even in old age, Pearl could still focus on more than her own needs and conveniences. She was willing to forgo the added security of a grandson nearby if it were better for him and his family to live elsewhere.

Harriet and Pearl share more than their view of life as sacred vocation and their hearty laughter. They are each women of faith, rooted in their respective religious communities. Apart from genetic gifts, the spiritual sustenance each receives from her religious heritage may be a significant factor in their graceful old age.

In his book *The Healing Power of Faith,* geriatric psychiatrist Harold Koenig summarizes the mounting evidence that faith like Harriet's and Pearl's has been good for their physical and spiritual health. Koenig writes, "Treating patients over the years, I've seen many people's later lives blighted by chronic anxiety and rancor, a bitter, ongoing disappointment. They feel isolated and useless; the decades spent at work and raising their families now seem bleak futility." Dr. Koenig then draws this contrast, "But a large proportion of elderly people . . . are cheerful, optimistic, and seem to radiate inner peace and satisfaction with their lives . . . these emotionally tranquil older people often possess a strong religious faith, which they practice through regular prayer and congregational worship."[2] Other researchers have also found that in statistically significant proportions those elderly persons whose world is given meaning through their faith and participation in a religious fellowship cope better with the physical losses of aging.

When he was in his eighties, Howard Thurman, one of our nation's great churchmen and human spirits, observed, "It is a hard thing when you get old to keep your horizons open. The first part of your life everything is in front of you, all your potential and promise. But over the years, you make decisions, you carve yourself into a given shape. Then the challenge is to keep discovering the green growing edge."[3]

How spiritually healing it is when older people can continue to grow, learn, and relish new experiences. Many universities now have programs of continuing education geared to those with greater leisure. I know persons with impaired sight who devour audio books, and I love to hear about "senior adults" who keep looking up new words in the dictionary or strive to acquire a new skill like crocheting or painting.

My Aunt Scotta, now in her late eighties, continues to expand her understanding of the world. Scotta Karff is a survivor of pancreatic cancer. Her eyesight is quite limited. When her sight became limited she began listening to audio books on the Bible, the history of England, and whatever else interested her. She enjoyed discovering classics she had never read before. When I call her long distance, she will invariably share something new she has learned about her world and her voice resonates with the excitement of fresh discovery. Her caregivers also became her teachers as she learned about their native cultures and personal stories. Aunt Scotta has certainly kept her horizons open in this last stage of life.

Thanks to advances in medicine and technology and our knowledge of nutrition and diet, we are generally living longer than earlier generations and many of us are able to do our aging with considerable vigor and vitality.

We admire those who continue to play respectable tennis in their seventies and eighties, whose mental agility remains notably intact, and whose physical demeanor is strikingly attractive. Indeed many of us are able to live mentally, physically, and socially active lives much longer than our ancestors. We are able to enhance God's world by our deeds even as we can take more time to enjoy the fruits of our labors and to savor the physical, intellectual, and aesthetic delights of living.

But if brokenness goes with the territory we call life, old age is its favorite nest. Some negotiate the pitfalls with less visible scars than others, but as death is an inexorable price of life, physical wearing down is the price of aging. Some die before encountering chronic disability but none who lives long is spared the price of longevity.

The time comes when a hearing aid no longer fully compensates for the degeneration of the auditory nerve. The eyes need larger print, or because of macular degeneration, we may no longer be able to read at all. Sexual vigor has become a wistful fantasy. Short-term memory may be severely impaired. Resistance to dozing in the presence of a luncheon speaker is a lost battle. And even that last symbol of independence, our driver's license, has been surrendered.

Aging brings multiple losses. While the disabilities of living long affect us at different levels and rates of intensity, none can escape the loss of energy and of faculties we once took for granted.

A religious perspective proclaims that at each stage we are accountable, have deeds to perform, and possess gifts to bestow. And at every stage, God cherishes us unconditionally. Viewing our physically diminished self through this lens of faith enables us to love ourselves in our brokenness.

This challenge is not easy and may be most difficult for those who have acquired and lost "celebrity status." British actor Alec Guinness told of his last encounter with actress

Beatrice Lillie. Lillie, whose exuberant vitality and physical charm once had made her the center of attention and interest at every social gathering, was now dealing very badly with the ravages of age. When Guinness approached her at a glitzy New York party, she dismissed him with the words, "I'm just not worth speaking to. Forget me."[4]

For the famous mime Marcel Marceau, Charlie Chaplin was a much admired model and icon. Marceau tells of his only encounter with Chaplin at an airport terminal building. He noticed the legendary Chaplin bent over, his frail frame supported by a cane in the arm of a companion. What a radical contrast with the incredibly nimble performer who enthralled audiences and was one of the best-known, most admired artists of his time. Marceau hesitated to intrude upon Chaplin but could not resist the opportunity to meet him. Chaplin recognized the name Marceau and after they spoke briefly they shook hands and parted. But Marceau noticed that tears streamed down Charlie Chaplin's cheeks, perhaps in sad awareness that Marceau was probably the only one in that terminal building who recognized him.[5]

In the minds of Beatrice Lillie and Charlie Chaplin the loss of celebrity status was linked to the loss of bodily suppleness and vigor—the toll of old age. No doubt coming to terms with the loss of celebrity is painful and requires some grieving. Those of us who have lived less public lives are spared that harsh adjustment. But many reach midlife or retirement to face the painful awareness that they did not fulfill some or many of their cherished dreams. Moreover, they must acknowledge that those dreams will not be realized. This awareness can trigger feelings of painful failure that erode a sense of self-worth.

If we are obsessed with what we did not achieve, we may undervalue the significance of the life we have lived. Even well-known, accomplished people are not immune. Astronaut Bill Thornton is a physician, physicist, and engineer who not only visited outer space, but also helped NASA to overcome the engineering challenges of conducting experiments in a weightless environment. Dr. Thornton, now retired, lamented to me how little he managed to accomplish compared with what he could and should have done. I was both stunned and amused by his assessment of an unusually accomplished life, but he meant it.

Many persons tend to underestimate the significance of their lives. I delight in helping them revalue their achievements in the family and in the world at large. I want to help them see that their life resumés are far richer than they have realized. Nevertheless, the brokenness of body and of unfulfilled dreams is a reality for all of us in one way or another. We need to do the grieving for those losses. That, too, is part of healing.

In time, we must strive to move beyond grieving. Sally Gadow speaks of old age as a time "to cultivate a conscious integrity of self and body, . . . to care for it as one would a beloved with whom one has laughed and danced and from whom one soon will be parted."[6] That task is not easy, but my capacity to love my broken self may be strengthened by the unconditional love of dear ones and by my faith in the healing, loving presence of my Creator.

The losses thrust upon us by aging are a great challenge to the spirit, especially when these irreversible changes threaten us with isolation and portend the approach of the angel of death. I wonder how well I will confront the disabilities of aging that may radically constrict my world.

At such times I think of Joe Sittler, a beloved congregational minister who in later life became a professor of theology at the Divinity School of the University of Chicago. He was so devoted to his students that he once refused an invitation to an out-of-town conference because, in his experience, Chicago's bleak December was when his students most needed his counseling.

At eighty-three, long retired, his wife deceased and his children scattered, Joe Sittler lived alone, largely confined to home because of complete blindness and frailty. He did not sentimentalize his isolation. A year before he died, Dr. Sittler addressed a conference in which he characterized life with elegant simplicity, "Life has a term, it unfolds its inward possibilities, and then it closes."[7]

Still, Joe Sittler continued to be warmed by the memory of so many joyful and meaningful moments in his life's journey. He could still smell the flowers that friends brought to him and remember their radiant beauty. He was comforted by his favorite biblical texts and classic prayers and his soul continued to be stirred by classical music. All who visited him encountered a man who faced the waning of his life with sadness tinged with courage and leavened by faith.

When the physical brokenness of old age severely restricts us we need God's unconditional love and that inalienable worth derived not from what we do but from who we are. But what of the active dimension of the covenant that calls us to be a blessing? Can we still bestow blessings even as we await our death? My memory of Barbara and of Larry enables me to answer affirmatively.

Barbara lived a privileged and gracious life. She was a beautiful woman who found her Prince Charming in her husband Harold. An exceedingly devoted couple, they enjoyed each other and the camaraderie of lifelong friends. They traveled widely, raised children, delighted in their grandchildren, and were blessed with good health and prosperity during much of their adult years.

Barbara spoiled her grandchildren and lent her time, enthusiasm, and great organizational skill to raise significant sums for numerous causes in our community, among them the Campaign to End Hunger.

At the end of her sixth decade, Barbara was stricken with an illness that progressively immobilized her and was life threatening. Valiantly she continued to enjoy the company of friends and family. She appeared at parties, restaurants, and her synagogue. Harold was her ardent comforter, encourager, and wheelchair pusher. After the medical modalities had been exhausted, Harold and the family were determined to care for Barbara at home and make whatever time was left as comfortable as possible. Barbara knew her days were numbered.

I visited with Barbara one day when she was confined to her bed. Heavily sedated, she alternated between sleep and wakefulness. Her grandchildren took turns lying next to Grandma, to stroke her arm, kiss her, and tell her of their love. In moments of alertness she took every opportunity to express love for each member of the family.

During the last week of her life, Barbara managed to perform a great deed. She became the healer of a rift within the family. Knowing how she craved family solidarity, the estranged parties who visited her deathbed became reconciled. So it may be said that to her last moment of conscious life she not only experienced the healing balm of love, but the satisfaction of healing a rift in the lives of her dear ones.

Larry also taught me that those who await death may have precious gifts to bestow. In his sixties he came to our city to be near his children and grandchildren. A few months after the move, a malignant tumor was discovered and, despite surgery and chemotherapy, the destructive process was irreversible. Larry was dying and he knew he was dying. Although his body was progressively consumed, his mind was intact.

When it became evident that Larry would not live to witness his grandson's bar mitzvah, I arranged a brief ceremony with a Torah scroll in his room at the nursing home. Larry's grandson read the Torah and recited the *Sh'ma* prayer in his grandfather's presence. I blessed the lad, but Larry gave him the most powerful blessing as he kissed and hugged his grandson, smiling through his tears.

Once Larry asked me, "Rabbi, how do you prepare for this?" I thought of the rabbinic dictum that we ought to live each day as if it were our last. "Larry," I said, "We should prepare all our lives, and you have prepared well. You show your love and care. You have a sense of right and wrong. You've made your share of mistakes like the rest of us but you've earned a good name. You will be missed. Maybe this is your finest hour and your greatest gift to your family: You've accepted your dying with sadness, but not bitterness—and with great consideration and appreciation of your family's kindness. I pray when my time comes I have half your courage and integrity. It is a privilege to know you." I hugged him and assured Larry how much he had blessed me.

Throughout our days we live in a tension between an awareness of our power and our fragility. We are held accountable for the responsible use of our power and we are loved unconditionally by our Creator even in our brokenness. This is the essence of our covenant with the Source of our being.

Whether we are old or young, physically and emotionally healthy, or chronically ill, we experience the strength and frailty of our human condition. From the perspective of faith, at each stage of our conscious existence we are asked, "What are you doing this day to repair and heal my world?" We are also called to welcome the loving embrace of our Creator and to realize that at each stage of life, God confers upon us the gift of meaning.

Chapter 11

Dance, Laughter, and Hope

There is hope for your future. —Jeremiah 31:17

L IVING WITH MY WIFE for more than four decades I have come to appreciate dance, which the dictionary defines as "rhythmic and patterned bodily movements usually performed to music." Dance has been a core activity and passion of my life partner since her childhood. The love of modern dance was passed on from her mother to Joan, and while it seems to have skipped a generation, there is still hope for my grandchildren.

I am one of those nerds who never took a dance lesson, so I ended up marrying a dancer. Ever since our engagement forty-two years ago I have been receiving informal instruction from a most talented and long-suffering dancing partner. As I write these words, Joan is in another corner of our cottage where she plays her tapes and choreographs for the modern dance company she founded and has directed these past twenty-five years. Occasionally I am conscripted to model a pose or movement she has created. At wedding receptions, Joan is so adept at compensating for the deficiencies of her partner that when we leave the dance floor people actually compliment us.

I'll never forget a particular wedding reception that we attended many years ago. A year earlier, the parents of the bride had faced the loss of a son who was killed in an accident while serving in the Peace Corps. At the time of the wedding the bride's father was battling an undiagnosed muscular ailment that impaired easy mobility and clouded his future. Yet, despite this somber backdrop—or perhaps because of it—the bride's parents danced at their daughter's wedding with intensity and joy. They were savoring the present moment with all their "heart and soul and might."

I was reminded of that occasion when I opened the *New York Times* Sunday magazine and saw the photograph of a beautiful young girl in a party dress. She was standing on a table encircled by glasses of wine and people clapping their hands as they watched her. A lone woman remained seated at the table. She, too, was clapping as she gazed lovingly at the girl. This accompanying text by thirteen-year-old Maggie Burrows told the story:

> I was at my bat mitzvah. . . . My mom unfortunately has a brain tumor and multiple sclerosis, so she couldn't really dance. She was sitting down. The D. J. walked over to her, and everyone followed. I don't remember why exactly I got on the table, but suddenly I was jumping up and down, the glasses were splashing all around. . . . Other people won't remember it, but it was just the most magic moment for me.[1]

The ancient rabbis were not familiar with the terms "sound bite" or "bumper sticker," but at times they reduced the complexities of the Torah to its underlying core. Thus Rabbi Simeon once suggested that all 613 commandments in the Torah are contained in the simple declaration, "The righteous shall live by his faith (Habakkuk 2:4)."[2] When the sage Hillel was once asked to summarize the imperatives of his faith, he responded, "What you don't like, don't do to your neighbor. . . . The rest is commentary."[3]

Shrewdly Hillel added this admonition, "Go and study it." That was Hillel's way of acknowledging the danger of over-simplification or, as we would say, the peril of trying to capture the essence of a religious faith on a bumper sticker. Yet as we move toward the conclusion of this book let me suggest three gifts that are inextricably bound up with a life of faith. These gifts are encoded in the words *dance, laughter,* and *hope.*

Simchat Torah is a festival observed each fall at the conclusion of the Feast of Tabernacles *(Sukkot).* It marks the completion of the annual reading of the Torah in the synagogue and the beginning of a new cycle. We read the last verses in Deuteronomy, recounting the death of Moses as the Israelites approach the promised land, and begin again with the opening verses of Genesis, the story of the world's creation.

On *Simchat Torah,* Hasidic Jews not only read from the Torah but physically embrace the sacred scrolls and dance with them. This custom has spread even to the more decorous Reform Movement. In virtually all synagogues today, *Simchat Torah* (which means rejoicing with the Torah) includes a congregational processional of dancing with the Torah scrolls.

To dance is to fully enter the present moment with full attention and surrender to joy. A Hasidic tale describes what it means to dance: One *Simchat Torah* eve, Rabbi Mendel watched his faithful dance holding the scrolls of the Torah. They seemed so distracted by their burdens that their movements lacked intensity and passion. Clearly their minds were not in sync with their bodies. This lack of *kavanah* ("attention" or "focus") troubled the rabbi so much that he interrupted the dancing. "That's not the way to dance!" he commented, looking angry. "Imagine yourself on a mountain peak, on a razor's edge, and now: dance, dance, I tell you!"[4]

The bride's parents at that wedding and Maggie Burrows at her bat mitzvah were not Hasidic Jews and yet they got Rabbi Mendel's message. Good dancing requires a full engagement of body and mind with no holding back of energy; a total commitment to what you are doing at the moment, not permitting your awareness of life's troubles to deflect you from the precious joy of the present. On the contrary, that awareness may only intensify the full savoring of the present moment.

For Rabbi Mendel, dancing on a mountain peak on a razor's edge was a metaphor for life. Life is a dance and we are the dancers. So often we bring to the dance a consciousness of past burdens and looming trials. How easily we may be distracted by our worry agendas. If we fail to focus mind and energy on the possibilities of the moment, our life lacks intensity, passion, and joy.

Perhaps the rabbi's disciples were so weighted down by dark uncertainties that they could not savor the present moment or be open to its grace. Rabbi Mendel was exhorting them: given the contingencies in our lives we are all dancing on a razor's edge, but that is all the more reason to do our dancing with the fullness of our being.

To be sure, our life is not all we would want it to be. Too much is pending or unresolved. If only we could leave town for that glorious vacation with all our problems neatly wrapped up back home. If only we could attend our child's graduation without the burden of a job change or future surgery hanging over our heads. If only we could celebrate a daughter's wedding unburdened by the lingering sadness of a recent death or an undiagnosed ailment hovering over our future.

In truth, we all live with baggage from the past or the anxious burdens of an uncertain future. One of our children may be doing well while another is going through a difficult crisis. And so we tell ourselves, "You are only as happy as your least happy child." A couple is about to celebrate twenty-five years of happy marriage but their family business has been far worse than last year. Life does not permit us to forget for long that we are dancing near the edge of a cliff. But that is all the more reason to enter the dance of life with the fullness of our being. One of the saddest tricks we play on ourselves is to imagine all the menacing contingencies that could at some point assault us, only to deny ourselves the accessible blessing of life today.

One evening my wife and I were discussing Rabbi Mendel's tale. That night Joan dreamed she was visiting a friend in a multileveled townhouse. One level contained a huge Caribbean colored swimming pool, framed by the lush landscape of a tropical isle. The water was buoyant like the Dead Sea. In a distant corner of the pool she noticed several rust-brown, tentacled creatures. When Joan's face became knotted in fear, her host assured her that if she relaxed and trusted the water and enjoyed the pool the creatures would not bother her. Joan relaxed and trusted the water. She floated effortlessly and enjoyed an amazing moment of bliss and then awoke. When Joan relayed the dream to me neither of us required an interpretation.

If in that dream those tentacled creatures had made menacing gestures and seemed poised for attack, Joan could not be expected to swim blissfully. But so often when we worry about possible threats in our future, we only keep ourselves from savoring the real joys of the moment. Therefore, we ought not be like the Parisian lawyer in Albert Camus's novel, *The Fall,* who confesses, "I was absent at the moment when I took up the most space."[5] We must not permit the burdens from our past or the uncertainties of our future to keep us from joyfully embracing a grandchild or dancing fervently at a wedding or watching a sunset with the fullness of our being.

To find meaning and healing in a world that is both troubling and glorious we must not wait until the Messiah comes—and all perplexities are resolved—before we dance with fervor and joy. For if we do wait for all perplexities, past or future, to be resolved, we only cheat ourselves without lightening our burdens or the burdens of others. The wise person will savor the joy in life with an intensity and gratitude that is only deepened by the awareness of life's brokenness.

Dancing through life with full presence is one sign of a sustaining faith; laughter is another. The Talmud tells of Rabbi Beroka of Khuzistan. The prophet Elijah appeared to him in the marketplace, perhaps in a vision or in one of the disguises the prophet used for his earthly visitations. The rabbi asked Elijah, "Is there anyone in this marketplace who is to have a portion in the World-to-Come?" Without hesitation Elijah pointed to two men in the crowd. Rabbi Beroka confronted the men, "What do you do?" he asked. They replied, "We are clowns. When we see people depressed, we cheer them up."[6]

Quite often the jester uses laughter not only to ease our pain but his own. A deeply distressed man went to see his physician. The doctor could find no physical ailment. Before dismissing his patient the doctor said, "I recommend that you go to the circus. There you will find a clown whose name is Grimaldi. He will cheer you up." The patient looked up at the doctor and said plaintively, "But doctor, I am Grimaldi."

Some years ago at our family Seder, one of the guests wisecracked intermittently and touched our funny bone. The laughter was good; after all, the Seder is intended to be more celebratory than solemn. The jester's words helped to distract the woman at our table from thinking of her aches and pains. She told him so afterward. As it turned out the man who made us all laugh that night had some months earlier experienced the tragic death of a young daughter. He made us laugh in part to ease his own pain.

A study of fifty-five of America's leading comics reveals that the vast majority of them combated an inner sadness through their humor. Syndicated columnist and premier humorist Art Buchwald is a case in point. His mother died when he was an infant and his father placed him and his three sisters in foster homes, which the father visited each week on Sunday. During his first sixteen years of life Art lived in seven households. Making himself and others laugh has been Art Buchwald's way of healing his hurt.

Vaclav Havel became president of Czechoslovakia after the collapse of the Soviet Union. The castle on the hill in Prague, occupied successively by Czech kings, Hapsburg emperors, and Communist party bosses now became the office of a Czech playwright whose defiance of the previous regime had earned him time in a dank prison cell. Catapulted from the role of artist and dissident to leading statesman, Havel presided over a community in the throes of difficult and dangerous transition. Political power did not dim his literary sense of irony or his appreciation of the gift of laughter. "It's difficult to explain," wrote Havel, "but without the laughter we would simply be unable to do the serious things. If one were required to increase the dramatic seriousness of his face in relation to the seriousness of the problems he had to confront, he would quickly petrify and become his own statue."[7] Life, Havel contends, is too serious to be lived without the balm of laughter.

When I visit a person imprisoned in a massive cast and likely to remain so for a month or more, and that person greets me with a humorous comment and some laughter, I take such laughter as a sign of momentary triumph over disability.

The same is true of the infirmities and disabilities of old age. Some of us simply bemoan our fate, some futilely resist it, others are able at least part of the time to laugh about it. I fondly remember Henrietta Bowman, whom I used to visit at the nursing home. Henrietta never married. In her earlier years she enjoyed a successful career as an insurance executive. Then in her nineties, confined to a wheelchair, hard of hearing and no longer able to read even with her magnifying glass, Henrietta would reflect on the deterioration of her body with a hearty, boisterous laughter. I took her laughter not as a sign of disrespect for herself or denial of the realities of her life, but as a triumph of her human spirit. Visiting Henrietta was not a chore but a privilege.

In the difficult days after lightning and fire destroyed our home, I personally experienced the healing power of laughter. A few days before the fire I had been playing tennis. One of my shots perched momentarily on the net before rolling over to the other side. Chiding me about my luck, my opponent threw up his hands in mock despair and complained, "What can you do when you are playing against someone with special connections up there!" My standard response to such claims is, "I'm in sales, not administration." A few days after he heard of the fire, my tennis partner greeted me at our Sabbath worship service with the words, "You're right, you really are in sales, not administration." We both laughed.

The following week I looked at my pocket calendar and discovered a bonus of free time the next Wednesday afternoon. That was the time I had scheduled to meet with an expert on expanding the bookshelf space in my study. With no house, I no longer needed new bookshelves for my study. "Well," I declared to my secretary, "That's one meeting I don't have to go to." With that quip I achieved a momentary triumph over the new circumstances of my life.

In his book *The Culture of Pain,* David Morris notes the verse from the book of Proverbs, "A merry heart doeth good like medicine."[8] Some version of this credo was prevalent well into the eighteenth century. Then, Morris notes, the theory of therapeutic laughter lapsed into oblivion, until more recently there has been a new emphasis on psychosomatic and holistic medicine. Morris detects a major turning point when *The New England Journal of Medicine* published Norman Cousins essay titled "Anatomy of an Illness (As Perceived by the Patient)." In that essay Cousins described his debilitating illness, "The bones in my spine and practically every joint in my body felt as though I had been run over by a truck." With the encouragement of his physicians, Cousins watched videos of entertaining programs like *Candid Camera.* Laughter substantially relieved the physical pain and helped him resist melancholy.

What empowers us to enter the dance of life with "heart and soul and might"? What enables me to savor the tight embrace of a granddaughter and become playfully engaged in her world? What underlied Henrietta Bowman's laughter in the face of the progressive wearing-out of her body?

Dance and laughter are ultimately religious statements. They attest to a primal faith that chaos, suffering, and evil, do not speak the final word in the cosmos. They bear witness to God's presence. Dance and laughter express the soul's insistence that in spite of everything there is meaning and value in our life journey. Dance and laughter bear witness to a God who is the creator and sustainer of the world, the one who reveals the way we are intended to live, and who is with us as our ultimate companion and reliance.

In other words, dance and laughter are rooted in hope. We see this connection between laughter and hope in the biblical story of Isaac's birth and naming.

When Abraham and Sarah heard from the angel of God that they were to be blessed with a child, they laughed. Abraham laughed as he said to himself, "Can a child be born to a man a hundred years old, or can Sarah bear a child at ninety?" (Genesis 17:17). "Sarah laughed to herself, saying, 'Now that I am withered, am I to have enjoyment—with my husband so old?' " (Genesis 18:12).

But the promise of the angel was fulfilled. The baby was born and named Yitzhak (Isaac), which in Hebrew means "laughter." Sarah says, "God has brought me laughter; everyone who hears will laugh with me" (Genesis 21:6). The laughter of scorn and self-mockery is transformed into the laughter of hope renewed and the joy of fulfillment.

This child would not be spared life's trials. He would endure the trauma of his near-sacrifice at Mt. Moriah, but he survives and prevails. Yitzhak does live to experience the joy of continuing the covenant, the joys of love, marriage and parenting—and the joy of blessing his descendants.

Hope is based on trust that God our Creator, guide, and helper remains actively and lovingly present in our lives. The opposite of hope is despair. Hope is often a struggle against despair because life tests us, it challenges us; life demands that we leave the comfort of the known for the unknown. Life denies us final victory. It does not permit us to freeze precious moments or to hold on to what we now have and cherish. Hope is a necessity and a struggle because in every life there is a sense of absence of something we want but do not have or something precious we once had but have lost. In

every life there is bitter defeat and disappointment, brokenness of body and spirit. No one is immune from experiencing
the "dark rim edging the sunlight."

There are times in every life when hope languishes and
despair threatens to overwhelm us. Still, faith reminds us that
despair is never permitted to speak the last word. Many of us
have discovered that if we face the depth of our fear and
anguish and move through the storm and the darkness we
can emerge to the sun with an even deeper understanding of
the preciousness of life and living. From our encounter with
the pit, from having stood on the very rim of death, we can
experience the profoundest kind of hope for life.

The Hebrew word for hope, *tikvah*, comes from the root
"to wait." Hope is our expectation that pain, defeat, and bitterness are not the final words in our lives. The psalmist
waits for God as "the watchmen [wait] for the morning"
(130:6). The watchman has spent a long night but he waits
expectantly for sunrise. The psalmist explains, "One may lie
down weeping at nightfall; / but at dawn there are shouts of
joy" (30:6).

Hope is linked to the promise of the future. In many an
oppressive situation the Jew has remembered the story of the
exodus and dared to hope that the God who redeemed Israel
from Egyptian bondage "will redeem me from the bondage
in my life." Much of Jewish faith is oriented to the future.
The prophet Jeremiah counseled his exiled people with the
words "there is hope for your future."

God's world is not yet fully redeemed. We do not live in
messianic times of perfection. But we live with hope that
tomorrow may bring some release and partial fulfillment
even if the fullness of redemption is at the end of days. Many
of us can testify to such redemptive or "messianic moments."
In the midst of illness we may experience the miracle of

restored good health; when we are buffeted by inner conflict and great anxiety, we may discover unexpected courage to face life with energy and joy. When we have been bruised by betrayal in the matters of the heart, we may in time rediscover the power to love again; when we have been assaulted by the indignity of vocational dislocation or economic uncertainty, we may discern new opportunities to use our gifts and to care for the needs of our family. And, in the midst of the mixed bag that is life, we discover our power to savor the dance of the moment and to burst into hearty laughter.

At such moments some of us may say or at least feel that God is with us. Equally significant is the discovery that in the midst of great trouble, we can somehow muster the strength to face another day. Many years ago a man in my congregation described his tangled feelings after receiving a diagnosis of lung cancer. When he left my office that day I reconstructed his words because I knew I wanted to keep them:

> Suddenly as the fact hits you, you find yourself spinning in all directions, meaningless. Round and round you spin in perpetual motion. Then in time somehow the spinning slows down. You begin to see shapes and forms, you begin to see tasks and responsibilities, you begin to feel some ground under your feet. Somehow the gyroscope is working again. You are able to carry on; things to do, persons to care about—and you continue the journey with fear and hope.

I learned recently of this man's death—thirty good years after he had spoken those words.

Ellen, a charming, outgoing woman, was in the hospital for chemotherapy. A glitch had developed which made her arms black and blue and caused much discomfort. This was not directly related to her cancer and the chances of it happening were one in a thousand. She was depressed and found herself asking, "Why me?" Such a question was rare for her though she had struggled with cancer for a number of years. I called and asked if I could visit. She normally did not like visitation during her trips to the hospital but almost eagerly she asked me to come.

Ellen began by telling me that her sister prays regularly, is a believer, and is helped by prayer. Her sister wanted her to talk to me about getting more help from her religion. Ellen told me, "I'm grateful for my sister, my friends, the miracle that my daughter and I are speaking again and that my sister and I are closer than we have been in the past. I'm grateful but I can't address words to someone or something that's not there. I'm not sure that 'it, he, or she' is there. I guess I'm an agnostic."

"Ellen, you are more spiritual than you realize," I told her. "You've had so much to endure in your life: a difficult divorce, estrangement from a child for which you blame yourself, and you manage to get up and face each day with zest and courage. You've also felt all alone through some of that struggle but you've found the strength to do what you needed to do. You are also grateful for your many blessings. You just haven't permitted yourself to name the God who appeared to you."

We smiled at each other with an understanding, respect, and affection fostered over years. I continued, "As a sophisticated woman it is difficult for you to commit to that which can't be seen or 'proved,' yet you don't live by pure rationalism. You've told me you are going to beat the statistics. You believe you are going to lick this cancer. All the doctors give you is the probabilities and those statistics are not encouraging. Your expectation is an act of faith. You live with hope."

I was suggesting that Ellen's hope was based on a faith that goes beyond reason alone. This faith could not be proved or disproved in a laboratory. It was not based on statistical probability and could not be dismissed as a form of denial. This "hope against hope" empowered Ellen to keep fighting for her life.

As I prepared to leave I told Ellen how deeply I respected her spirit, guts, and sense of humor through it all. With eyes misted over she said, "Your coming here today when I so needed you must be more than a coincidence; it's very important to me." As I left, with a twinkle in her eyes and a radiant smile, she said, "I thank God for your coming."

Many of us have heard the expression "as long as there is life, there is hope." This suggests that as long as I live, despite whatever assails me, there is a possibility I shall prevail. We know, however, that death is as real as life and at times, despite all the hope that has sustained us in our battle for life, we are rapidly, inexorably slipping away. We know we are dying. What hope can be sustained at such a time?

Life is a continuous drama of separation and connection. We fulfill our deepest human need when each separation is followed by some reconnection. The baby in the womb experiences life's primal separation, followed—under the best of circumstances—by nursing at the mother's breast. Later on the first day of nursery school the child will face a more extended separation. Under the best of circumstances this trauma will be followed by meaningful connections to the teacher and some of the child's peers and by a reunion with parents later in the day. The process is reenacted when the college student leaves home and subsequently, when the young adult, like the biblical Adam, "leaves his father and mother's house and cleaves to his wife."

The anticipation of our dying represents the most fateful separation of all. At death we disconnect ourselves from this life; there is no return and we carry nothing away. What can we hope for at the end of life? My wife and I recently visited

Mackinac Island, Michigan, where horse-drawn carriages and bikes are the only conveyances. We biked around the island on a road framed by the crystal clear waters of Lake Huron on one side and a pristine forest on the other. As we stopped to savor a particularly scenic spot, I noticed a sign with the words "Take Nothing But Pictures; Leave Nothing But Footprints."

Those words offered me a powerful metaphor for the last leg of my own life journey. I dare to hope I will be leaving some substantial footprints of my walk on this earth. I hope there will be lives that reflect my influence. I want to be remembered and missed. I want to face separation from this world with confidence that the footprints I leave behind will preserve my vital connection to it.

When he was professor of Medical Humanities at the Galveston Branch of the University of Texas Medical School, my friend Tom Cole led a group of older adults. They met to write and share aloud their life stories. One participant in the workshop explained that "we are paying attention to ourselves . . . to what we have done and been and lived through." Another said, "Your life is a bunch of stories, and then you put it down, and it has form. You think, 'This is my life and it is O.K.' "

A *New York Times* journalist who wrote an article about such story-writing groups explains, "These new memoirists are writing for the same reasons writers have always written: to search for the meaning in their lives, to find their voice, to leave a record."[9] This story-writing enterprise is at heart a sustained effort to validate the meaning of one's life on this earth, "I have not lived in vain, I will leave this earth knowing that I will be remembered and missed."

Most of us tend to underestimate the impact of our lives. When I counsel people who have reason to believe their lives are ebbing they will often lament the meagerness of their accomplishments. I encourage them to share with me those things of which they are most proud. I help them recognize and recount those events and influences that have made their lives significant. Often they will be surprised by their own attainments and by the many ways they are likely to be missed and remembered within and beyond their families.

When Morrie Schwartz, the hero of Mitch Albom's *Tuesdays with Morrie,* was confined to his room with ALS, he knew his life was ending. He recalled the funeral of a dear friend and the nice words spoken by the minister. It bothered him that his deceased friend could not hear those words. So Morrie decided to stage a living funeral for himself. He invited his close friends to his room one Sunday afternoon and asked them to speak about him as they would after he died. The living funeral was a great success. His friends spoke with deep feeling and humor. All present laughed and cried—including Morrie.

I am not advocating that we duplicate Morrie's ritual but I have seen the spiritual healing in the misty-eyed face of a dying friend as I sat with him and recounted what he meant to me and others and how his life had touched and ennobled us. Many of the same words would later be spoken by me at the funeral.

At the end of life the only hope some of us can muster is the assurance that we will have made a difference and will be missed—and will thereby remain connected to this world. And that hope may be sufficient. But faith offers a still deeper hope in the presence of death. The psalmist said, "Where can I escape from Your spirit? / Where can I flee from Your presence? / If I ascend to heaven, You are there; / if I descend to Sheol, You are there too" (139:7-8). And in Ecclesiastes we read, "Dust returns to the ground / As it was, / And the lifebreath returns to God / Who bestowed it" (12:7).

Despite its burdens and travails, life on this earth is precious, unique, and to be cherished. Therefore, many of our expectations do rightly center on this life. As long as we can, we hope that God will remove our earthly troubles or empower us to live with them. At best, however, our days are numbered, "They are speedily gone and we fly away." Can we hope that beyond our death and beyond our footprints on earth something of us will remain? Will the essence of our being, our soul, our spirit be sustained eternally by the Source of all creation?

For many years such belief seemed hopelessly unmodern. Many Jews even asserted that Judaism does not believe in an afterlife. Such is hardly the case. Judaism refrains from speculating too much on the details of our postmortal destiny or the "geography" of heaven, but it nevertheless affirms that death is not the end of human life. The philosopher Maimonides observed that for us to understand the notion of the beyond is like a person who is born blind trying to grasp the nature of color. Still as we stand at the grave of a loved one we recite, "We praise You, Adonai our God, Ruler of the universe, who forms us in the divine image, who nourishes and sustains us in Your goodness, who causes all of us to die, and who implants immortal life within us. We praise You, O God, Judge of truth."[10] Thus Judaism nourishes the hope that the separation from earthly life is followed by our return to the Source of our being.

In an age of science many immediately dismiss the notion of life beyond death as a flagrant violation of the laws of physics, while others have attempted to make a scientific case for immortality. Physicist and philosopher Danah Zohar describes an immortality based on quantum physics, "In a quantum view there is no way to draw any sharp distinction between my persistence through time, my close relationship to others, and my survival after death. Neither isolation nor death has a clear cut meaning . . . in the language of quantum physics."[11]

Grounding immortality in the language of the latest science may make it more acceptable for some, but the notion that death is real and God is its conqueror preceded the new and old physics by many centuries. My religion teaches that in death the soul returns to the Soul of the universe who preserves all that is good from destruction.

The philosopher George Santayana referred to immortality as the soul's "invincible surmise." At age seventy, when Rabbi Alexander Schindler retired from the presidency of the Union of American Hebrew Congregations, he reflected on Santayana's words:

> The death of my beloved father . . . awoke in me the intuition that death is a portal rather than a sealed wall. . . . How could all that animates life—the capacity to know, to create, to love, to dream—be snuffed out like a sputtering candle . . . ? The reawakening of spring after winter, the miracle of birth from the inner space of our bodies, the constant transformation in exchange of matter and energy—all these testified against the idea that death meant obliteration rather than transformation. Thus it was that my "surmise" began to attain its "invincible" force.[12]

I like best the metaphor for immortality used by the twentieth-century Jewish mystic, Rabbi Abraham Isaac Kook. He viewed our life on earth as an inverted tree with its roots in heaven. The trunk and the branches of the tree represent our deeds on earth while its roots are in God.[13] The more we are nourished by the roots in this life—the more we fulfill God's commandments and cultivate our relation to our creator—

the more soul we will bring to the Soul of Souls after our days on earth have ended. Such is the other kind of hope Judaism offers me as I contemplate the end of my days.

What of those whose life is snuffed out in early childhood or infancy before they have had an opportunity to live a full life and cultivate their souls? This circumstance is addressed by the ancient rabbinic statement that some persons acquire eternity in a lifetime of striving and doing while others acquire eternity in a single moment. I referred to that teaching at the graveside service for seven-year-old Nicholas. The God I believe in does not deny eternal life to those who, through no fault of their own, were denied the privilege of a long life.

Ronny Finger was not denied enough years to make a difference in the world. He knew he was a blessing. In an earlier chapter, I cited Ronny's affliction at age sixty with ALS. The day he came to recount the diagnosis, I assured him I would try to be with him and help him draw strength and hope from his religious faith. When I encouraged him to share his thoughts and feelings, he expressed gratitude for many wonderful years of life—for family, friends, achievements in business, and service in the community. His life had certainly been good, but he hadn't expected it to end just yet.

Ronny feared isolation from friends and total dependency upon others for his needs. I tried to assure him that his true friends would not abandon him and that he would somehow be able to handle the dependency. Subsequent events vindicated my assurances. His friends did stand by Ronny with amazing steadfastness. About thirty men met Ronny for lunch at his favorite Chinese restaurant as long as he was able. These "Wednesdays with Ronny" were a balm to his spirit. Ronny also continued to go out with friends and enjoy their company even when he needed to be fed by an attendant.

Before we parted that day, Ronny asked me if we Jews believed in life after death. More specifically, did we believe that there was more to immortality than the deeds and memories we leave behind? He listened intently to my response and seemed palpably comforted by Judaism's belief in the soul's eternal life with God.

During Ronny's eighteen-month journey I always concluded a visit by reciting the Priestly Benediction ("May the Lord bless you and keep you . . .") and by kissing his forehead. One day, while he could still speak, he whispered, "I want to live as long as I can handle it and I am ready to go when the man upstairs calls me." Ronny found comfort in both the assurance he had blessed the lives he touched on this earth—and in the trust that his final separation from this world would be followed by a reconnection to the Soul of the universe.

Harriet Goldstein was a woman in her fifties when she died. She had lived with cancer for more than two decades: remission, recurrence, treatment, remission, recurrence elsewhere in the body, treatment until she was told there were no more therapeutic modalities but more experiments could be tried. At that point Harriet had had enough and asked only to be kept comfortable.

The Sabbath afternoon before she died I happened to be visiting her. It was a period of clarity and alertness between morphine applications. Harriet was not denying her impending death; she had come to terms with it. Her life had been good. She was sad but not bitter that she had lost the battle with cancer. She now only prayed that the end would come soon.

I asked Harriet what she was thinking at this time. She related an incident from her childhood when she and her sister had been brought to the hospital for the removal of tonsils. Harriet was five years old, her sister two. Mother held the hand of each daughter. Since Harriet was older, she was asked to go first. She pleaded with her mother to go with her. Mother insisted she must remain behind with the younger sister, but she assured Harriet that she could trust the nurse who at that moment had taken her hand and was leading her through a doorway to an unknown land. Later, when Harriet awoke, she saw her mother and realized that all was well in this new land.

That episode came to Harriet's mind now as she prepared to make her journey to an unknown land. She quipped that while I had often spoken of eternity as a realm of peace and a state of perfect serenity, she hoped for more action in the world beyond. Harriet expressed trust in the Source of being. She was grateful for all she had experienced in her life, including the love of her husband and children and the joy of grandchildren. Following this half-hour interlude Harriet dismissed me as courteously as she could and we said *shalom*. That was the last time I saw her before conducting her funeral service.

When we suffer the loss of a loved one we are impelled to consider the meaning of his or her life and our own. We grieve our loss and come to terms with the starkest reminder of our own mortality. What comfort and hope is there for those of us who are left behind?

When my mother died, I who had comforted others now found myself on the mourner's bench. I learned that feelings I had helped others deal with were suddenly mine, including guilt. After I learned of my mother's precipitous failing, I rushed home, but I arrived only in time to kiss her lifeless form. We had been in touch by long-distance phone daily during those intervening days and she knew I loved her and that I would be coming back soon. She was not alone in those final days and hours, but I was not there with her.

For my feelings of regret I received the proper responses, "You gave her so much joy. . . . She shared so many wonderful times with you and your family. . . . You really said good-bye when you kissed and embraced her three weeks earlier. . . . How could you know?" Still the added pain and regret hurt deeply. Mine was not a perfect good-bye, which only highlighted the more momentous truth: for all our precious bonding we did not fulfill all of each other's expectations. Ours was not a perfect relationship; perhaps there are none.

During the time when grief mingled with gratitude and regret, I received comfort from my loving family and friends. I was consoled by my mother's rabbi and by his fitting tribute filled with genuine fondness and respect for this truly remarkable woman. I found comfort in the cantor's chanting of the *El Maley Rachamim* (a special prayer for the dead), in my recitation of the Kaddish, and in the tears, smiles, and hugs of all who tried to help me cope with my loss.

In the weeks following I became more viscerally aware of God's great gift of maternal love, more keenly mindful of the jagged edges in all our relationships, and more appreciative of the gift of forgiveness from each other and from the One who has taught us to reach beyond our grasp. From my own days of mourning I also learned the wisdom of our tradition: Do not return immediately from the grave to the stream of life. As Murph, my philosopher friend from the Health Club said, "Rabbi, you ain't no child to no one no more." Whatever our age, it is not easy to realize we are orphans. Stepping aside from life for a while, as tradition prescribes, was my declaration that an awesome event had assaulted me. I could not simply do business as usual. I had crossed a threshold and things would never be the same.

The weeks following the funeral taught me not only to come to terms with the finality of mother's death but to feel in a new way the reality of her abiding presence. At the funeral the rabbi had said she reminded him of a book titled: *Saying Goodbye without Leaving.* In her lifetime she touched me so powerfully that her spirit would abide. I remain connected to her. Anecdotes continually pop into my mind. Her favorite expressions still punctuate my speech. I don't need photographs or videocassettes to conjure her image. Even unbidden, my mother's strong, nurturing, at times brooding presence is as close to me as my breathing. Her soul is not only eternally in God's keeping; her life spirit abides within me to bless me, my family, and all who were touched by her life.

It is not the same as it once was. The loss is real. The pain is real. But so is the vivid presence in my mind and heart. What is our most precious consolation at such a time as this? The confident hope that those who have given us life will in some way continue to accompany us on our journey. We are helped by the thought that they lived well and by the belief that their death is a return to the Guardian of Eternity.

Hope sustains us as we face our own mortality or grieve for one who has departed. That hope is embodied in the rabbinic story of an old man crouched close to the earth as he planted a little sapling of a carob tree. A Roman general sauntered by and challenged the worth of his labors. "Old man, of what use is this planting? You will not live to eat of this tree's fruit!" The old man replied, "If not I, then my children and my children's children will eat of this fruit."[14]

Our hope for immortality may focus on being remembered by our descendants and in having made a difference in the lives of those who will mourn and remember us. This hope lies in the trees that have been planted, the memories created, the footprints left behind. But my heritage also proclaims that second hope: since God is the ultimate conserver of what is precious and most to be valued, death is a return to the Source of our being. That which is best in us and our loved ones will abide because God remembers us and God permits death no victory.

Hope's firm root is faith that the Source of all being—the one to whom we return in death—also walks with us in life. This faith empowers us to embrace life—to cherish its delights and to bear its burdens—because we are embraced by the Giver of life.

Notes

Preface

1. Martin Buber, *Tales of the Hasidim: The Early Masters* (New York: Schocken Books, 1947), p. 228.

Introduction

1. Elie Wiesel, *Somewhere a Master* (New York: Summit Books, 1982), pp. 11-12.
2. André Malraux, *Antimemoirs,* trans. Terence Kilmartin (London: Hamish Hamilton, 1968), p. 1.

1. What Is Faith?

1. This is my translation of Pinhas of Koretz, *Imray Pinhas: The Sayings of Pinhas* (Tel Aviv: Ehrenberg and Frankel Publishers, 1974), p. 162.
2. Viktor E. Frankl, *Man's Search for Meaning: An Introduction to Logotherapy* (New York: Simon & Schuster), pp. 56-57.
3. Genesis Rabbah 22:9 (Hayim Nahman Bialik and Yehoshua Hana Ravnitzky, eds., *The Book of Legends: Sefer Ha-Aggadah* [New York: Schocken Books, 1992], p. 101).
4. Abodah Zarah 54b (I. Epstein, ed., *Hebrew-English Edition of the Babylonian Talmud: Seder Nezikin* [London: Soncino Press, 1935], p. 279).
5. Moses Maimonides, *The Guide of the Perplexed,* trans. Shlomo Pines (Chicago: University of Chicago Press, 1963), pp. 443-44.
6. Kiddushin 39b (I. Epstein, ed., *Hebrew-English Edition of the Babylonian Talmud,* p. 195).

7. Bialik, *The Book of Legends,* p. 247, ¶ 205. Beruriah quotes Job 1:21.

2. What Kind of Life Is This Anyway?

1. Adin Steinsaltz, *Simple Words: Thinking About What Really Matters in Life* (New York: Simon and Schuster, 1999), p. 213.

2. Joseph H. Hertz, *Sayings of the Fathers: Pirke Avot* (New York: Behrman House, 1945), p. 77.

3. Ta'anith 21a (Hayim Nahman Bialik and Yehoshua Hana Ravnitzky, eds., *The Book of Legends: Sefer Ha-Aggadah* [New York: Schocken Books, 1992], pp. 230-31, ¶127).

4. Ibid., p. 230, ¶126.

5. David Polish, ed., *Rabbi's Manual* (New York: Central Conference of American Rabbis, 1988), pp. 90-91. Used by permission.

6. Vayigash 3 (Yaakov Culi, ed., *The Torah Anthology: MeAm Lo'ez,* vol. 3, trans. Aryeh Kaplan [New York: Maznaim Publishing Corporation, 1977], pp. 480-81).

7. Rachel Naomi Remen, *My Grandfather's Blessings: Stories of Strength, Refuge, and Belonging* (New York: Riverhead Books, 2000), p. 78.

8. Jim Valvano, "ESPY Award Address," delivered March 4, 1993, www.americanrhetoric.com/speeches/jimvalvanoespyaward.htm.

3. Confronting the Obstacles to Faith

1. Saul Bellow, *Mr. Sammler's Planet* (New York: Viking Press, 1969), p. 313.

2. Tanhuma 7 (Hayim Nahman Bialik and Yehoshua Hana Ravnitzky, eds., *The Book of Legends: Sefer Ha-Aggadah* [New York: Schocken Books, 1992], pp. 509-10).

3. Ecclesiastes Rabbah 7:13 (Francine Klagsbrun, *Voices of Wisdom* [Middle Village, N.Y.: Jonathan David Publishers, 1980], p. 452).

4. Garret Hardin, *Nature and Man's Fate* (New York, Rinehart, 1959), pp. 306-29, quoted in Ralph Wendell Burhoe, *Science and Human Values in the 21st Century* (Philadelphia: Westminster Press, 1971), p. 170.

4. Recovering Faith—A Guide to a Deeper Spirituality

1. James Atlas, "The Art of Failing," *New Yorker Magazine* 74, no. 13 (May 25, 1998): 70.

2. Saul Bellow, *Henderson the Rain King* (New York: Penguin Books, 1996), p. 24.

3. Samuel E. Karff, "Life's Traumas Bless Us with Faith," *The Houston Chronicle* (February 5, 1995): C49.

4. Elie Wiesel, *Souls on Fire: Portraits and Legends of Hasidic Masters* (New York: Summit Books, 1972), pp. 203-5.

5. Herman Gollob, *Me and Shakespeare: Adventures with the Bard* (New York: Doubleday, 2002), p. 20.

6. Ibid., p. 23.

7. Baba Bathra (I. Epstein, ed., *Hebrew-English Edition of the Babylonian Talmud* [London: Soncino Press, 1935], pp. 14a-14b).

8. Hagigah, chapter 1, Halacha (*Hagigah and Moed Qatan*, vol. 20 of *The Talmud of the Land of Israel: A Preliminary Translation and Explanation*, trans. Jacob Neusner [Chicago: University of Chicago Press, 1986], p. 32).

9. Leon Wieseltier, *Kaddish* (New York: Alfred A. Knopf, 1998), pp. 25-26.

10. Clifford Geertz in *The Religious Situation*, ed. Donald R. Cutler (Boston: Beacon Press, 1968).

11. Abraham Joshua Heschel, *The Earth Is the Lord's* and *The Sabbath* (New York: Harper Torchbooks, 1966), p. 75.

12. Herman Wouk, *This Is My God: The Jewish Way of Life* (Boston: Little, Brown and Company, 1987), p. 45.

13. Natan Sharansky, *Fear No Evil*, trans. Stefani Hoffman (New York: Random House, 1988), p. 272.

5. Prayer—The Vital Connection

1. George Dennis O'Brien, *God and the New Haven Railway: And Why Neither One Is Doing Very Well* (Boston: Beacon Press, 1986), p. 132.

2. Martha Beck, *Expecting Adam* (New York: Berkley Books, 2000), p. 290.

3. Jeff Levin, *God, Faith, and Health: Exploring the Spirituality-Healing Connection* (New York: John Wiley & Sons, 2001), pp. 181-82.

4. Ibid., p. 182.

5. Eugene B. Borowitz, *Studies in the Meaning of Judaism* (Philadelphia: The Jewish Publication Society, 2002), p. 347.

6. Paraphrased from Rosh Hashanah 18a (I. Epstein, ed., *Hebrew-English Edition of the Babylonian Talmud* [London: Soncino Press, 1935]).

7. Elie Wiesel, *Somewhere a Master* (New York: Summit Books, 1972), p. 16.

8. Martin Buber, *Tales of the Hasidim: The Later Masters* (New York: Schocken Books, 1948), p. 277.

9. Nina Beth Cardin, "The Dew of Life," *Outstretched Arm 5*, no. 1 (Fall 1995). *Outstretched Arm* is a publication of the National Center for Jewish Healing, New York.

10. See Larry Dossey, *Healing Words: The Power of Prayer and the Practice of Medicine* (San Francisco: Harper San Francisco, 1994), pp. 169-95.

11. David A. Cooper, *A Heart of Stillness: A Complete Guide to Learning the Art of Meditation* (Woodstock, Vt.: SkyLight Paths, 1999), p. 10.

12. Ibid., p. 17.

13. Ibid., pp. 208-9.

14. Ibid., p. x.

15. Menahoth 43b (I. Epstein, ed., *Hebrew-English Edition of the Babylonian Talmud*).

16. *Paths of Faith: The New Jewish Prayer Book for Synagogue and Home,* trans. Chaim Stern (New York: S.P.I. Books, 2003), p. 106.

17. Kenneth Prager, "For Everything a Blessing," *Journal of the American Medical Association* 227, no. 20 (May 28, 1997): 1589.

6. Overcoming a Crisis of Faith

1. Arthur Green, *Tormented Master: The Life and Spiritual Quest of Rabbi Nahman of Bratslav* (Woodstock, Vt.: Jewish Lights Publishing, 1992), p. 291.

2. Ibid., p. 296.

3. Hullin 3b (Hayim Nahman Bialik and Yehoshua Hana Ravnitzky, eds., *The Book of Legends: Sefer Ha-Aggadah* [New York: Schocken Books, 1992], p. 511, ¶59).

4. Berakoth 33b (Bialik, *The Book of Legends,* p. 522, ¶139).

5. One translation of this Scripture that I especially like is Sheldon H. Blank, *Jeremiah: Man and Prophet* (Cincinnati: Hebrew Union College Press, 1961), pp. 9-11.

6. Sidney Greenberg and Jonathan D. Levine, *Mahzor Hadash: The New Mahzor for Rosh Hashanah and Yom Kippur* (Bridgeport Conn.: The Prayer Book Press of Media Judaica, 1978), p. 84.

7. Gittin 56b (I. Epstein, ed., *Hebrew-English Edition of the Babylonian Talmud* [London: Soncino Press, 1935]).

8. Elie Wiesel, *The Gates of the Forest,* trans. Frances Frenaye (New York: Holt, Rinehart and Winston, 1966), p. 198.

9. Rabbi Gerald I. Wolpe, Excerpt from High Holy Day Sermon Booklet.

10. Alfred North Whitehead, *Religion in the Making; Lowell Lectures, 1926* (New York: Macmillan Company, 1926), pp. 16-17.

11. Abraham Joshua Heschel, *A Passion for Truth* (New York: Farrar, Straus, and Giroux, 1973), pp. 272-73.

12. Ibid., p. 273.

7. When Prayer Is Not Enough

1. Berakoth 5b (I. Epstein, ed., *Hebrew-English Edition of the Babylonian Talmud* [London: Soncino Press, 1935]).

2. Carl C. Jung, "Psychotherapy and the Clergy," *Psychology and Religion: West and East,* vol. 11 of *Collected Works,* trans. R. F. C. Hull (New York: Bollingen Foundation, 1958), ¶509.

3. Zion's Herald. "ZH Interview: Lauren Artress." Zion's Herald (March 2001), p. 2; www.zionsherald.org/March2001_interview.html. Zion's Herald is published bi-monthly by the Boston Wesleyan Association.

4. *Gates of Prayer: The New Union Prayerbook* (New York: Central Conference of American Rabbis, 1975), p. 625.

5. Martin Buber, *Tales of the Hasidim: The Early Masters* (New York: Simon and Schuster, 1982), pp. 268-69.

6. Berakoth 5b (I. Epstein, ed., *Hebrew-English Edition of the Babylonian Talmud*).

7. Harlan J. Wechsler, *What's So Bad About Guilt?* (New York: Simon and Schuster, 1990), p. 36.

8. The Power of Love

1. Elie Wiesel, *Somewhere a Master* (New York: Summit Books, 1982), p. 108.

2. Edith Wyschogrod, *Saints in Postmodernism: Revisioning Moral Philosophy* (Chicago: University of Chicago Press, 1990), p. 150.

3. Sara Rimer, "The Fate of Flight 800: The Afteraffects; Using One's Own Anguish to Help Others," Late Edition, *New York Times* (August 19, 1996): B1.

4. Anatole Broyard, "Dr. Talk to Me," *New York Times Magazine* (August 26, 1990): 146.

5. Anthony Burgess, *A Clockwork Orange* (New York: W. W. Norton and Company, 1986), pp. 126, 83.

6. Hayim Nahman Bialik and Yehoshua Hana Ravnitzky, eds., *The Book of Legends: Sefer Ha-Aggadah* (New York: Schocken Books, 1992), p. 12, ¶45.

9. Living in a Broken World

1. H. Jacob Freedman and Maurice Simon, eds., *Midrash Rabbah* vol. 2 of *Genesis Rabbah* (London: Soncino Press, 1983), pp. 729-30.

2. Pesikta Rabbati 6.7 (Hayim Nahman Bialik and Yehoshua Hana Ravnitzky, eds., *The Book of Legends: Sefer Ha-Aggadah* [New York: Schocken Books, 1992], p. 125, ¶114).

3. Leonard Kriegel, *Falling into Life* (San Francisco: North Point Press, 1991), p. 6.

4. Norman Podhoretz, "On Being a Jew: Sidney Hook," *Commentary* (October 1989): 34.

5. Gerald L. Sittser, *A Grace Disguised: How the Soul Grows Through Loss* (Grand Rapids: Zondervan Publishing House, 1996), p. 34.

6. Ibid., p. 144.

7. Miriam Rosenzweig, *The Stories He Told: The Dubno Maggid on the Weekly Parashah,* vol. 1 of *Bereishis-Veyikra* (Southfield, Mich.: Targum/Feldheim Press, 1991), pp. 80-84.

8. Kriegel, *Falling into Life,* p. 85.

9. Podhoretz, "On Being a Jew," p. 34.

10. Sittser, *A Grace Disguised,* p. 104.

11. *Gates of Repentance: The New Union Prayerbook for the Days of Awe* (New York: Central Conference of American Rabbis, 1978), p. 329.

12. Alfred Kazin, *A Lifetime Burning in Every Moment: From the Journals of Alfred Kazin* (New York: Harper Perennial, 1997), p. 243.

13. Philip Roth, "Pictures of Malamud," *New York Times Magazine* (April 20, 1986): BR1.

14. Hayim Nahman Bialik and Yehoshua Hana Ravnitzky, eds., *The Book of Legends: Sefer Ha-Aggadah* (New York: Schocken Books, 1992), p. 103.

15. This is my translation of Mordecai HaCohen, ed., *Al HaTorah* (Jerusalem: Reuben Moss Publisher, 1962), p. 94.

16. Bialik, *The Book of Legends*, p. 249, ¶221.

17. Günter Grass, *Local Anaesthetic* (New York: Harcourt, Brace & World, 1969), p. 284.

10. Sustaining Faith in Our Later Years

1. Martin Marty, "Moving Aside Some Thoughts on My Retirement," *Park Ridge Center Bulletin,* no. 6 (October/November 1998): 15.

2. Harold G. Koenig, *The Healing Power of Faith: How Belief and Prayer Can Help You Triumph over Disease* (New York: Touchstone, 2001), p. 28.

3. Cited in Sam Keen, *Learning to Fly: Trapeze—Reflections on Fear, Trust, and the Joy of Letting Go* (New York: Broadway Books, 1999), p. 239.

4. Patrick O'Connor, "He Is Good for You," *Times Literary Supplements* (May 7, 1999): 186.

5. Scott Simon, "Interview: Mime Actor Marcel Marceau Discusses His Life and Work Then and Now," Weekend Edition, National Public Radio (January 29, 2000).

6. Thomas R. Cole and Sally A. Gadow, eds., *What Does It Mean to Grow Old?: Reflections from the Humanities* (Durham, N.C.: Duke University Press, 1986), p. 241.

7. Joseph Sittler, "Reflections on Aging," *Perspective,* adapted from the speech "How Does Our Society Today Value Aged Persons?" delivered at the Human Values Institute Conference, Madison, Wisconsin, May 12-14, 1986.

11. Dance, Laughter, and Hope

1. Catherine Saint Louis, "What They Were Thinking," *New York Times Sunday Magazine* (August 12, 2001).

2. Makkoth 23b-24a (Hayim Nahman Bialik and Yehoshua Hana Ravnitzky, eds., *The Book of Legends: Sefer Ha-Aggadah* [New York: Schocken Books, 1992], pp. 462-63, ¶567).

3. Bialik, *The Book of Legends*, p. 651, ¶126.

4. Elie Wiesel, *Souls on Fire: Portraits and Legends of Hasidic Masters* (New York: Summit Books, 1972), pp. 235-36.

5. Albert Camus, *The Fall* (New York: Alfred A. Knopf, 1982), p. 87.

6. Bialik, *The Book of Legends*, p. 713, ¶269.

7. Vaclav Havel, *Disturbing the Peace: A Conversation with Karel Hvizdala*, trans. Paul Wilson (New York: Alfred A. Knopf, 1990), p. 113.

8. David B. Morris, *The Culture of Pain* (Berkeley: University of California Press, 1991), pp. 94, 97.

9. Sara Rimer, "Turning to Autobiography for Emotional Growth in Old Age," Late Edition, *New York Times* (February 9, 2000): A14.

10. David Polish, ed., *Rabbi's Manual* (New York: Central Conference of American Rabbis, 1988), pp. 154-55. Used by permission.

11. Danah Zohar with I. N. Marshall, *The Quantum Self: Human Nature and Consciousness Defined by the New Physics* (New York: Quill/William Morrow, 1990), p. 149.

12. Alexander M. Schindler, "Dear Reader," *Reform Judaism* 24, no. 2 (Winter 1995): 2.

13. Herbert Weiner, *9 1/2 Mystics: The Kabbala Today* (New York: Holt, Rinehart and Winston, 1969), p. 271.

14. Leviticus Rabbah 25.5 (Francine Klagsbrun, *Voices of Wisdom* [Middle Village, N.Y.: Jonathan David Publishers, 1980], p. 167).